SCOTLAND'S
CLANS AND TARTANS

By the same author
TARTANS OF SCOTLAND
THE TARTAN SPOTTER'S GUIDE
THE TARTANS OF THE SCOTTISH CLANS
HOW TO WEAVE FINE CLOTH

SCOTLAND'S CLANS AND TARTANS

James Scarlett

WITH LINE DRAWINGS BY
ANGUS McBRIDE

SHEPHEARD-WALWYN

© James Scarlett, 1974, 1981, 1984.
First published Lutterworth Press 1975.
This amended edition printed and bound in Great Britain by
Biddles Ltd, Guildford and King's Lynn for
Shepheard-Walwyn (Publishers) Ltd, 26 Charing Cross Road,
Suite 34, London WC2H 0DH

ISBN 0 85683 077 1

CONTENTS

Appendices

ACKNOWLEDGMENTS

I should like to record a particular debt of thanks to Mr. D. C. Stewart for his help, encouragement and painstaking but always constructive criticism.

My publishers and I also wish to thank all those who have helped with picture research for this book and those who have granted permission for the use of illustrations which are their copyright.

Plate 7, the portrait of George IV in Highland dress, is reproduced by gracious permission of Her Majesty The Queen.

The following illustrations are reproduced by the kind permission of the copyright holders: Plate 1, Mr. Ian Strachan; Plates 2, 15, 16, 18, and 23, the British Tourist Authority; Plate 6 and the Oronsay tomb slab and Jacobite broadsword shown in Plate 9, the National Museum of Antiquities, Scotland; Plate 10, the Scottish United Services Museum; Plate 13, the Mansell Collection; and Plate 22, the Scottish National Portrait Gallery.

We are grateful to Mr. Eoin Macpherson for his help in arranging for the obtaining of a photo of the Charmed Sword from the Clan Macpherson Museum at Newtonmore, shown in Plate 9.

Thanks are due to the Arms and Armour Press, publishers of John Wallace's *Scottish Swords and Dirks*, for their help with illustrations.

Plate 4 was drawn for this book by Mr. Angus McBride, and Plate 19 is my own copyright.

We would also like to acknowledge the help given by the National Trust for Scotland, and to thank in particular Mrs. Hallifax-Crawford, the Trust representative at the Weaver's Cottage, Kilbarchan.

Mr. Ingles Buchan of Galashiels generously helped with the obtaining of tartan specimens.

LIST OF ILLUSTRATIONS

COLOUR PLATES

9

MONOCHROME PLATES

LINE DRAWINGS, DIAGRAMS AND MAPS

Line Drawings and Diagrams

Maps

Note

Three line decorations are used in this book. The first shows a procession of figures of varying historical periods, the second is an abstract design in the Celtic style, and the third portrays the memorial column at Glenfinnan where Charles Edward Stuart, Bonnie Prince Charlie, raised the Royal Standard on August 19, 1745.

FOREWORD

Large volumes have been written about most of the subjects which are merely mentioned in this book, so it follows that any attempt to cover the whole subject of the Scottish clans and their dress (not forgetting their weapons and their tartans) in the space now available must be an enterprise of the utmost foolhardiness.

Within the limits imposed, my aim has been to look at the clansfolk as people, not all blood-thirsty villains nor yet all Bonnie Prince Charlies, and their dress as something better than a fancy dress suitable only for comic turns on the music-hall stage or occasions of military pageantry.

A large part of the space has been devoted to tartan, simply because so little informative matter is to be had on this fascinating and worthy subject; most of the available books are no more than short clan histories with tartan illustrations and by perpetuating the idea that everything is already known about tartan do much to conceal its very real interest.

The little that I have attempted could not have been done without the help and encouragement of many friends. If I mentioned all of them, I would fill another book, but some at least must be named. First, Donald C. Stewart, author of *The Setts of the Scottish Tartans*, whose patient teaching over many years has, I think, borne some fruit. Second, Stuart Davidson, founder of The Scottish Tartans Society, who gave me free run of the Society's collection and records, thus enabling me to carry out my own research instead of merely copying the work of others. Third, the late Miss Alison Stewart, first Director of Research of the Society, a kindred spirit whose urging of me on to the completion of an earlier, still-born work, ensured that this one was ready when needed. It is to her memory that the book is, with respect and affection, dedicated.

The Gaelic of the clans was predominantly a spoken language, which gives some point to the saying 'It is a wonderful thing to have written a book, even a bad one.' This book would have been worse without the efforts of the editor, Miss Jenny Overton, and those others of the publishers' staff concerned with its production.

Authors' wives are incredible creatures, long-suffering, hard-working, able to find exactly the right word just when it is most needed, knowing when to speak and when to remain silent, helping to read proofs. Mine is all this, understands punctuation and sees my jokes as well.

James Scarlett
Edinburgh, 1974

My thanks are due to the Lutterworth Press, whose ready co-operation with Shepheard-Walwyn Ltd made this second impression possible.

J. S. Milton of Moy, March 1981

'These observations are, I trust, true on the whole, though I do not pretend to show that they are perfectly void of mistake, or that a more nice observer might not make any additions, since subjects of this kinds are inexhaustible.'

Gilbert White

SCOTLAND'S CLANS

THE CLANS . . .

Using round figures, we may say that the Highland clans flourished over a period of about five hundred years, commencing around A.D. 1200 and ending with the breaking of the clans after the Rising of 1745. During this period, hidden away in their inaccessible glens among the northern mountains, they were able to pursue their ancient and peculiar way of life entirely untroubled by the outside world, even at times when that outside world directed considerable effort towards their discomfiture.

When they left their own country, their dress and language marked them out as strangers, and their reputation at home was such that, until a very late date, any Lowlander who found himself obliged to visit the Highlands invariably made his Will first.

Even in the last years of the Clan era, 'pacification' (as it was called) of the Highlands was not a thing to be entered into lightly, and was usually planned at a safe distance, to be put into practice by others than planners. To the credit of those planners, we may still see, either as disused tracks across the hills, or in the lines followed by more modern construction, the network of military highways constructed in the years between the Jacobite Risings of 1715 and 1745; on the other side of the account, we have to take due note of the careful planning that went into the Glencoe massacre in 1692 and of the not entirely spontaneous atrocities committed by Cumberland's troops after Culloden in 1746.

'Clan' is a distinctively Highland appellation applied to groups of people who, regarding themselves as being all of one family, trace their descent from a common ancestor to whom, in the person of his rightful successor, all owe complete allegiance. 'Tartan', in the form in which we now understand it, was also a Highland development, and did not become popular for wear in the south of Scotland until it was used as a badge of protest against the Act of Union in 1707; after that its popularity increased, and before the end of the century it had come into common use, having at the same time developed into an extensive Lowland manufacture with a considerable export trade.

Inevitably, such a 'Lost World' as that of the Highlanders offered great attractions to writers, and from the time of Sir Walter Scott almost up to the present day, the clans and their tartans have provided favourite subjects for both the over-romantic and the over-critical; however, the modern trend towards a more realistic approach to history has at last given rise to the idea that there were both Galahads and bloodthirsty robbers among the old Highlanders, and so their history, their dress and their tartans have come to the fore as worthy objects for study. The result has been to make available a fascinating field of investigation, the more worthwhile for its being so nearly untrodden.

... HOW THEY BEGAN ...

It is tempting to think of the clans originating as settlers reaching a Promised Land, each group led by its Chief and Patronymic and all clad in their respective tartans, but reality does not match this attractive picture. Extant history shows the various clans to have had many different origins, love, war and royal favour all playing their parts, in accordance with the normal rules for advancement in those days.

For example, Somerled, the historical progenitor of Clan Donald, married a daughter of the King of Man who, as a vassal of the King of Norway, ruled the Hebrides. In due course Somerled first claimed, and then conquered, the Hebrides in the name of his eldest son; when he was assassinated in 1164, he left two sons, Dougal who founded the Mac-Dougalls, and Reginald, whose son Donald gave his name to the MacDonalds. Successful marriages and prudent politics enabled Donald's successor, John, to assume the title of Lord of the Isles in 1345. His sons, in their turn, formed branches of the main stem, Ranald founding the MacDonalds of Clanranald, Iain the MacDonalds of Kintyre and Islay and Alastair the MacDonalds of Keppoch. Ultimately the Lords of the Isles over-reached themselves, a not uncommon occurrence in those turbulent times, and the Lordship became forfeit in 1493.

More peaceful penetration was adopted by the MacFarlanes, named after Parlan, their fourth chief, but descended from a younger brother of the Earl of Lennox to whom the Earl gave a charter for the lands of Arrochar in 1230. Also of less violent origin are the MacNabs, who claim descent from the lay abbots of Glendochart in Perthshire, and the Robertsons, whose Gaelic name, Clan *Donnachaidh*, commemorates their first chief, Duncan the Fat.

In the wake of Malcolm III's English queen, Margaret, there came, in the late eleventh century, an influx of Anglo-Norman families with, probably, the Frasers, Chisholms and Grants among them; these too settled and became absorbed, first into the Lowlands and later, as they spread out in search of more land, into the Highlands as well.

Not every clan was large and powerful and so it often happened that

Map 1

Drawn in varying degrees of detail, and to varying standards of art, a map showing the territories occupied by the various clans appears in most of the tartan picture-style books, and although clans, like tartans, belong properly to the Highlands, these maps are nowadays generally extended to cover the Lowlands too and show the estates of the major Lowland families.

Upon occasion whole clans migrated, or were deported, but apart from these instances estates did inevitably change hands—for the clans were composed of people, *who moved around more or less freely, married into neighbouring clans, sometimes fought with them, bought from them, sold to them, even cheated them. Because of this, any map, however carefully compiled, can only be accurate for a given date and only remain accurate for a limited period. The detail differences that occur between one map and another do not, therefore, necessarily indicate that one of them is in error, but only that they relate to different times; however, it would still be unwise to rely absolutely upon a map of clan territories without having corroborative evidence.*

There is, nevertheless, a strong tendency for the old names to survive in the districts where the clans settled long ago. The name 'Cattanach', for example, which distinguishes a member of the Clan Chattan, survives in Badenoch, to which district many people of the 'Old' Clan Chattan emigrated at the end of the thirteenth century. Since there is at least some likelihood that the name was given to the incomers to distinguish them from the natives, there is a fair chance that this name has lasted there, in its birthplace, for six hundred years.

Similar examples can still be found, but it is possible that our own time will see the last of them, as the people move away to the industrial areas. Names live and survive only as long as there are men to remember and repeat them; a map record, however valuable, is a dead thing in comparison.

small clans would live upon the lands of the great chiefs, deriving protection from them and giving help when called upon to do so. In the last resort, ownership of land rested upon the ability to defend it, and so allies would be welcome as long as the land was sufficient for their sustenance; when congestion became too great, emigration was the only answer and so, from an early date, we find the Highlander thrusting out, perhaps as an explorer, but often as a soldier of fortune, a profession which brought high rank to many and left some notable 'Macs' among the European aristocracy, among them the Dukes of Taranto (MacDonald) and the Barons of Ophemert (MacKay).

The ones who remained at home formed the rank and file of the clan regiments in time of war, and even after the end of the clans, clung together to give the Highland regiments of the British Army a distinctly clannish background.

Today, although the clans no longer exist as units of society, Highlanders the world over, however many generations they may be removed from their homeland, recognise kinship with others of their name, and the tie seems to strengthen rather than weaken with time and distance. Clan Societies are active and some of them such as the Macphersons at Newtonmore and Clan *Donnachaidh* at Bruar in Perthshire, maintain headquarters and museums in their original country; these naturally have a special attraction for visiting clanspeople, and perhaps do a little to show the more casual tourist something of the past life of the Highlands.

The Clans died on the battlefield of Culloden, but much of their spirit lives on in the generosity and kind-heartedness of the Highlanders, especially evident towards the stranger among them; in these days their quarrels are more likely to be about shinty than over disputed ownership of cattle, but this can be blamed on progress.

... AND THE PEOPLE WHO MADE THEM

What kind of people were they then, these Highlanders who knew no laws but those made by their own chiefs and acknowledged no kings but of their own royal line? Travellers in the Highlands brought back alarming tales of their ferocity and general lack of civilisation and we cannot doubt that there was an element of truth about these; however, from Roman times until quite recently the use of a different language has been sufficient to mark a man as a barbarian, and even in these supposedly enlightened times, the word 'foreigner' has a slightly sinister sound.

The Chief of the Clan ruled it absolutely, with power literally of life and death over his people and over any enemies who might fall into his hands. Justice was rough and prompt and, there being no prisons, there were no prison sentences; according to rank, the guilty—or, we must admit, often the merely unlucky—went quickly to the heading pit or the hanging knoll (the past presence of the latter is indicated with great frequency on the modern map under the Gaelic name *Tom na Chroiche*).

Whether or no generations of such rough justice can be held responsible is difficult to say, but certainly among Highlanders a word was a bond, and although it would be rash to claim that they are unique in this, it was and remains a part of the national character. Allied to it is the tremendously strong tradition of hospitality which can surely only have been born and nurtured in small communities where a stranger was something so rare as to be specially cared for. There appear to have been no very firm rules of hospitality, but there are cases recorded of bitter enemies being given protection on claiming it, while its abuse was a dire thing, enough to keep Glencoe unfriendly towards a Campbell for nearly three centuries. A story told by James Logan in *The Scottish Gael*, and quoted by James Grant in *The Tartans of the Clans of Scotland*, gives point to this: in the seventeenth century, young Lamond of Cowal (this was the spelling of Lamont fashionable in Logan's time) killed the only son of MacGregor of Glenstrae, and fleeing from his pursuers, came running into the MacGregor's house, not knowing whose it was, and claimed protection. This the old laird gave, and would not break his word when he learned that Lamond had killed his own son; instead he fulfilled his pledge, even helping the young man to escape during the night. One of the variants of this tale adds that when the MacGregors were later being hunted down, Lamond of Cowal, now the chief of his clan, took old MacGregor of Glenstrae under his own protection.

Less desirably, the fierce pride in clan and race, and the fiery temper that went with it, had much to do with the bloody feuds that were part and parcel of clan life; albeit, though, to have pride in oneself and one's ancestry is not of itself a bad thing and pride in clanship was based on the belief that all were related to the chief (this was by no means always true, but it was believed, and that was what counted). It produced a society which was far from being a democracy, but one in which the barriers were vertical, between clans, rather than horizontal, between classes; whatever inequalities of wealth existed, all members of a clan held themselves of equal birth.

Apart from objecting to their inability to speak English, our early travellers were loud in decrying the indolence of the Highlanders and reserved a good deal of disfavour for their habit of lifting cattle from their neighbours. The Highlander of today is not noted for rushing about either, but gets where he wants just the same, arriving not out of breath and having had some time to think about what he is going to do when he gets there. As to cattle-lifting, the Highlands were largely devoted to raising cattle for the Lowland and English markets, and in these conditions cattle-lifting was as inevitable as was rustling in the later Wild West; in any case, with no welfare state, a bad harvest meant steal or starve. It may be added that lazy, trigger-happy cattle-thieves would not have left the marks of agriculture that remain, albeit overgrown with bracken, high in the mountains of the Highlands. Really hard work was necessary for survival, although the social structure of the clans prevented any change of status for the individual; perhaps in this we have the reason for the apparent lack of ambition in the Highlander; for those who stayed on the land ambition had no purpose. It has almost always been the returned emigrant who showed drive.

Even if lacking in ambition, our clansman did not lack ingenuity or

26

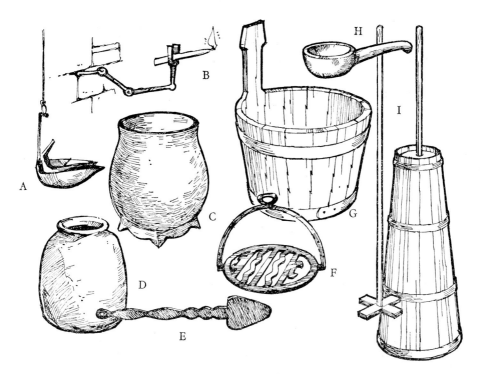

Fig. 1: Cottage utensils. A, a cruisie (an oil lamp); B, a holder for fir candles; C, cast iron pot; D, earthenware pot; E, bannock spade; F, girdle; G, porringer; H, ladle; I, butter churn and plunger

the skill to put it into practice, and folk museums abound in examples of his work. In an age without shops and with no travelling merchants except the occasional tinker, everything that was needed had to be made on the spot, and items such as domestic vessels made of narrow timber staves, the edges feathered together, are eloquent of their makers' skill.

Highland textiles, too, were noted for their beauty and fineness, and although we shall be seeing later that the tartan patterns that we have today are generally not as old as some would wish us to believe, the type of design is old enough and the colours used in earlier times have something that nobody has put into the synthetically produced colours we now use.

On the other side of the coin, the protection racket was invented by the Highlanders long before there were any American gangsters to think of it. It was the custom among some of the more lawless clans to levy what was called black mail (black meaning illegal, and mail meaning tax) upon their neighbours, the idea being that if the tax was paid, the neighbours' cattle would be protected; the reverse being equally true, though not mentioned, the Government raised, in 1667, the first of the Highland Independent Companies to act as military police especially in the way of making black mail an unhealthy occupation. New companies were raised in 1725, and at Aberfeldy in 1740 these were embodied into the 43rd Regiment, the first Highland Regiment of the British Army; in 1749 the regiment was re-numbered the 42nd, and is now famous as the Black Watch, the name being derived, we now believe, from its original duties as a watch, or police force, against black mailers, and not from the dark tartan that the regiment now wears.

WHAT THEY LIVED IN . . .

If the travellers showed themselves unimpressed by the Highlanders, their feelings in regard to Highland homes were no less marked. Unflatteringly, they called them 'hovels' and 'black houses', and it must be admitted that to a town-bred person, who was probably meeting true country dwellers at close quarters for the first time, such descriptions may have appeared quite apt. Observers were inclined to take exception to the sharing of the same roof by animals and their owners, forgetful of the fact that the animals were precious and needed protection, while the humans were well capable of taking care of themselves. Extremes of luxury and discomfort existed side by side in a gentleman's household in quite late years; Doctor Johnson remarks, with what sounds like a fair amount of disgust, that once on his tour in 1773, when delayed by missing a passage, he was given an elegant bed with fine sheets—but when he undressed, felt his feet in the mire.

Black these houses may have appeared from a distance, with their low stone walls and the roofs either thatched with heather or covered with turf; black they certainly were inside, for the peat fire that was the only source of heat for cooking, and therefore burned all the year round, was sited in the middle of the 'human' end of the house and the only escape for its smoke was through a hole in the roof. Although in course of time the fireplace migrated to the gable end, and a proper chimney was developed, until well after 1745 the usual type of small house consisted of low double stone walls with the space between filled with earth, and a roof made of light timber framing supported on pairs of main rafters, called 'couples', and either covered with thin turves laid like tiles or thatched with heather. The whole roof was firmly roped down with ropes twisted from heather roots and anchored to large boulders or stones left projecting from the walls for this purpose. This ancestry can be traced today in many a Highland cottage standing long and low at the roadside, a chimney at each gable end and its roof covered with slates.

In the early days, houses of more than one storey were so rare as to be automatically classed as 'castles', and the true fortified castle was

somewhat tardy in making its appearance in the Highlands. In general design, these early strongholds were stout rectangular buildings of stone built in mortar, three or more storeys in height, but still having gable-ended thatched roofs, a serious defensive weakness since to drive out the defenders, it was only necessary to lodge in the thatch an arrow with a piece of burning material attached; Carn ban Castle in Glen Lyon was disposed of in this way quite soon after the death of its builder, from which it can be argued that the life of this type of castle could not be expected to be long. Indeed, with few exceptions (such as the erstwhile home of the Wolf of Badenoch at Garth, which stands near General Wade's Military Road from Aberfeldy to Tummel Bridge, just north of Coshieville, and has recently been converted into a dwelling), the remaining castles of this type are either ruins or have been incorporated into later construction.

As time passed, and the great families of the Highlands became greater and consequently richer, grander edifices arose, and where these did not incorporate the old towers, the earlier building was either demolished or simply abandoned to the elements. This phase of development gave us the continental style of castle with hanging turrets and conical roofs, which looks so much as if it had been taken straight out of a book of fairy tales, especially when, as is so often the case, it stands wreathed in mist and low cloud in some Highland landscape.

Defensively, most of these latter-day castles also lack something; the Highland men hadn't the patience necessary for siege operations and were disinclined to sit indoors when a battle was waiting to be fought outside, and so we don't always find a castle so situated as to be resistant to attack: Dunvegan, the MacLeod castle on the Isle of Skye, was, it is true, for many years accessible only by sea, but on the mainland it is far from unusual for a castle to be sited in open country—a 'castle' in name, but in fact a palace for a local potentate. Castle Menzies is a good example. (Plates 15 and 16, between pages 88 and 89, illustrate the comparison.)

Figure 2: an imaginative reconstruction of an eighteenth century cottage scene. These were the 'black houses' of the Highlands. Note the roof: the exterior would be turved or heather-thatched.

Sadly, there are no longer enough rich families to preserve all these fine dwellings; some are ably looked after by The National Trust for Scotland and others, Blair Castle for example, are opened to the public by their owners—and are well worth a visit; but the days of lords like the nineteenth-century Marquess of Breadalbane, who lived in state at Taymouth and there entertained Queen Victoria, are long over. This great palace, built on the site of an earlier stronghold at the eastern end of Loch Tay, had a chequered career as an hotel, a military hospital, and a Civil Defence training college, and survived—almost miraculously, when we stop to think of the virtual destruction of other buildings that have suffered government occupation—in a fine state of preservation, with its beautiful plasterwork and decorations intact. At the time of writing, it is a school for American children.

A castle that, according to a tradition that may not be entirely accurate, sheltered an earlier queen than Victoria, is the old Menzies seat at Weem; also taken over for military purposes, this castle in which Mary Queen of Scots is said to have delighted to stay, has been derelict since the end of the Second World War and only now is some attempt being made to render it watertight in preparation for turning it into a clan meeting-place and museum.

... AND HOW THEY LIVED

You may by now suspect that the lives of the clansfolk were not all fun and frolic interspersed with clan battles. Fun there was, but it had to be subordinated to the serious business of getting a living, and of all the battles, that against Nature was the hardest.

As a pastoral people, the clans had a hard time of it, for although there are many broad and fertile valleys, called straths, by far the greater part of the Highlands is anything but fertile, no more than a thin layer of soil covering the rock beneath. Nor is the climate helpful, being generally too wet with too little sunshine; so far south as Glen Lyon, the sun disappears behind the mountains of the Lawers Range in October and does not reappear until March, while after a hard winter snow may lie on north-facing slopes until late in June.

To some extent, the poverty of the land and shortness of the growing season were compensated for by wider cultivation; just as the horse-drawn plough can be taken to places where the tractor-drawn one cannot, so could the old-style foot-plough, the *Cas chrom*, reach places inaccessible to either, and signs of earlier cultivation abound in areas now given over to bracken and the ubiquitous Blackface sheep.

Although the higher ground was generally unsuitable for cultivation, it could often give good grazing for a time, when the snow had cleared from it, and so, in the spring, the young folk and the children would set out with the cattle and many of the household utensils for the shieling grounds, there to lead something akin to the idyllic life with which they are so often credited, while the cattle fattened for the market or the pot and gave good milk to be made into butter and cheese. The sites of the huts in which the people lived while at the shielings can be discovered in many a sheltered corrie, the ruined drystone walls still standing perhaps knee-high, clustered in little groups around some burn which provided the water supply.

On the lower ground during this time, preparations would be going ahead for planting: the ground dug over; the byres dug out for manure, and perhaps last year's thatch removed from the house-roof for the same purpose. In the Islands, the 'lazy beds' would be prepared by

Figure 3 : using the foot plough, called in Gaelic the Cas chrom *(crooked foot). It is known to be of ancient origin, but its suitability for use on small plots and thin soil enabled it to survive into our own century.*

laying out sea-wrack (sea-weed) and digging a trench along each side, throwing the earth on top of the wrack to give a raised and well-drained bed—an energetic task, whatever the result might be called.

Clan lands were held by the chief, who sublet to his sons and near relatives, who sublet in their turn; so it went on down to the lowest levels and everyone farmed *some* land and owed some service for it. Most often, the land was distributed on the runrig system in which a single holding would consist of several plots, widely scattered, an arrangement which greatly upset observers who, used to more conventional methods, failed to realize that with land populated to the limit of its food-producing capabilities, it was of the utmost importance that it should be shared out equally in quality as well as in quantity.

Oats and bere (a primitive form of barley) were the food crops, but a little land might also be saved for flax, for Highland linen enjoyed a good reputation in earliest trading times. Root crops were unknown, even as cattle fodder, and hay was poor, so the beasts fared ill in winter, having to subsist on what the humans could spare and the occasional bundle of straw. Knowing this, we can hardly afford to be sceptical of stories that cattle could become so weak during winter that they had to be carried to the shielings; we need not wonder either that their descendants, though small, are remarkably hardy; but it is perhaps a little surprising that their beef should be so tender and their milk so creamy and even that their disposition should be so gentle in spite of a rather fierce appearance.

Cattle destined for the great Lowland cattle-trysts would set out early, pursuing a leisurely way and fattening as they went (and incidentally leaving more grass for those that stayed behind) and with these on their way and the ground planted, there would begin to be time for other things in the lengthening days of early summer. In compensation for the shortness of the winter days, those of summer are extra long, and in that same glen which sees no sun from October to March, dusk and dawn come near to merging at midsummer. Now would be the time for fun and frolic and doubtless there was some measure of both, but there was also the supply of peat for the winter to be got in, some hunting and fishing to be attended to, and the wool to be plucked (not sheared) from the sheep—a now extinct breed akin to the Soay sheep of the St. Kilda Islands—ready for spinning, dyeing and weaving during the winter months. It is hard to believe too that the human race has changed so much that the women would not have had ready a list of pressing household tasks with which to occupy any leisure that their menfolk might have arranged for themselves.

And so through the summer to the harvest, such as it might be, then the grain to be dried and stored ready for grinding as needed, cattle to be slaughtered, as late as possible—but no good to wait until the need was greatest, for by then they would be too thin to be of any use.

Compromise had to be reached, and what could not be preserved had to be used up quickly; salt was so heavily taxed as to be beyond the means of the ordinary people.

As autumn drew on and into winter, there would be progressively less outdoor work; likely enough some of the young bloods would set out on some freebooting expedition and probably return fewer than they went, but this was truly the season of the *ceilidh*, when people gathered in the evenings in each other's houses and provided their own entertainment with songs and music and recounting the age-old tales and legends of the glens, night after night, until the lengthening of the days gave the signal to prepare to set off to the shielings again, and so begin another year.

CUSTOMS AND BELIEFS

Customs, beliefs and superstitions become mixed over the centuries and it is difficult, often impossible, to separate one from another or even to distinguish pure fable from a folk tale based on some actual happening; in Highland proverbs there are many references to the dire doings of the fairies which result from the failure to perform some necessary action, but even these cannot be taken at exactly their face value. Legend to the contrary, it is not the fairies who upset the twist in the yarn if the driving band of the spinning wheel is left on while it is not in use; this is simply due to the fact that the band stretches and no longer drives properly.

Good luck charms and ill omens have a place in all our lives, and the Highlands can supply a lengthy list of them. To turn in a sunwise direction was always a good way of going about things, whether it was a matter of setting the fishing boat on its course (when it would ensure a good catch) or of perambulating a wishing- or healing-well. The properties of medicinal waters could also be greatly enhanced if a piece of silver were dipped in before one drank, an appropriate charm being recited the while, and some clans owned stones or crystals which could confer safety in battle on those who drank the water in which they had been dipped.

Apart from action to be taken to improve one's fortune, there were many observances which had to be followed in order to ward off ill luck. At sea certain words might not be used—'minister', for example— and certain things had to be referred to by pseudonyms; the words to be avoided and the names to be used varied, however, from one place to another, which must have made for difficulty in conversation when boats from different places happened to meet out sailing. The taboo on the use of correct names also extended to the land: some of the old rhymes and prayers use the word 'angel', for instance, in place of 'fire'; and another good, and perhaps necessary, safety precaution was to refer to the fairy people as the 'men of peace'.

A hint of a religion much older than our own remains with us in the form of a faint but apparently persistent belief in the need for a blood sacrifice to appease the spirits of the Earth when a new building was erected. There have been reports of this practice having lasted until quite recent years, when an unlucky cockerel performed the necessary office, but legend has many tales to tell of buildings haunted by the ghost of some unfortunate wayfarer who was killed to be buried in the foundations. Legend has it also that St. Oran was buried alive in the foundations of Iona Cathedral for this purpose; on being dug up some days after, miraculously still alive, he delivered to his startled colleagues the opinion that Hell might well be a lot worse and that Heaven was not all it was cracked up to be, whereupon the scandalized monks hastily shovelled the earth back on top of him.

There is fascination in tracing legends to what seems to be a logical source and one particularly Highland creature gives an excellent opportunity of making the attempt. The Urisk (*Uruisg*) of legend is a water goblin, but it often happens that an urisk is associated with an early Christian missionary of similar name. A Glen Lyon site closely associated with St. Ninian has a 'grey goblin' (*bodach odhar*—literally a dun-coloured little old man); the picture that this and similar instances conjures up is quite vividly that of a hermit occupying his cell beside some convenient stream and working the occasional 'miracle' for primitive people who would naturally award him supernatural status in return. This impression is heightened by the frequent similarity between the names of the Urisk and the holy man—the Urisk Paldy, for example, seems to have lived quite close to St. Palladius.

There was one very nasty inhabitant of Highland waters, and that was the Water Horse. Although almost the only one left is the Loch Ness Monster, the number of Highland lochs that are associated with the creatures is considerable and shows that they were formerly believed to exist; Adamnan's *Life of St. Columba*, dating from about A.D. 700, relates that the saint encountered a water monster in the neighbourhood of Loch Ness, so the idea is not a new one. The amount of evidence of sightings is such that it cannot be claimed that the appearance of these creatures is entirely due to the observers taking too little water with it.

Whatever is in Loch Ness will, we hope, be one day revealed, but the water horse of folklore was a fairy creature, able to assume human form, in which it usually appeared as a handsome and well-dressed young man with the object of making love to unwary maidens and carrying them off to the depths of its loch. A wise maiden would always respond to such advances by running her fingers through the young man's hair; if this revealed bits of water-weed and grains of sand, she knew what she had to contend with. By this time her caressing should have put the water horse to sleep, and so she was able to escape quite easily. In its proper guise as a very fine horse, a water horse was wont to entice children to ride upon it; once mounted, they found themselves stuck and were thus carried off. A woman—and only a woman—could capture a water horse by stealing its bridle and substituting a cow's halter; she then had an exceptionally fine and hard-working horse, but it was now just a horse and somehow not quite so interesting as before. This theme has its counterpart in the Islands where, if legend is to be believed, many a man has won himself a bride by stealing the skin shed by a seal maiden when she has assumed, as she sometimes does, human form. In the stories, the skin is always hidden away by the husband, but the seal wife finds it in later years, thus being able to return to her own people; we have accordingly been deprived so far of proof of what might be a very interesting matter.

HIGHLAND DRESS

The earliest form of dress worn by the Highland men of which we have any useful knowledge was the **saffron shirt** (*Leine Chroich*) which was brought from Ireland by the Scots—an Irish tribe—who settled on the coast of Argyll in the seventh century A.D., and which continued in use until the closing years of the sixteenth century. This was a voluminous garment of linen, apparently much pleated, padded and quilted; the name indicates that it was yellow, but we have no means of telling if it was dyed with saffron, or was merely of 'saffron' colour. There is no indication what the indigenous Highlanders were wearing at the time; it has been suggested that they wore only tattoo marks, but these can hardly have given adequate protection against the rigours of the High-land climate, and the probability is that they had already adopted some type of covering, little, if at all, different from the **belted plaid** (*Breacan feile*) that eventually supplanted the saffron shirt.

The belted plaid was a piece of material about one and a half yards wide and six long (about 1.40 metres by 5.50 metres), made of two 'single' widths of material sewn edge to edge. It had to be made in this way because, prior to the invention of a mechanical means of throwing and catching the shuttle, a handweaver had to lean forward over the loom and put a hand at each side of the web in order to throw and catch, and this limited the width that could be woven to about twenty-seven inches (about 70 cm); the usual explanation of this, that the shuttle cannot be *thrown* any further by hand, is nonsense; a full-size shuttle will go quite a long way under the force of a gentle flip with the forefinger.

The belted plaid cannot have been a very convenient garment to put on quickly; one method, so we are told, was to lay it on the ground over a belt, pleat it to taste, then lie down upon it and do up the belt. M'Intyre North, whose *Book of the Club of True Highlanders* came out in 1882, was scornful of this, and contended that the only right way was to gather the pleats in the hand, pass the plaid round the body, and fix it with the belt, tightening this after a final adjustment of the pleats. Either method probably had its uses and whichever was adopted, the

40

Figure 4: it is difficult to believe that this method of donning the belted plaid would have worked well in an emergency, but on the other hand it is probable that in times of emergency it was never taken off.

result was a garment that was ideal in its time, the single piece of material serving as a kilt and what amounted to a cape that could be adjusted in as many ways as the weather called for.

41

Contemporaneously with the belted plaid, **trews** (*Triubhas*) were worn, though Sir John Sinclair contended that these were, in fact, the earlier dress, and they were certainly known in Ireland in the tenth century. Trews are a kind of trouser tailored to a tight fit, the material being cut on the bias to give the necessary elasticity, and they incorporate hose; it has been said before, but will stand repetition, that the tartan trousers called trews in the Army are nothing of the kind—they come in varying degrees of tightness, but genuine trews are *tights*. Later, there came pantaloons which look quite like trews when hanging in a museum showcase, but lack the built-in hose and are more like jodhpurs in cut.

In the Highlands, trews became, in course of time, 'gentlemen's' wear, being more suited to a horseman than was the belted plaid; out of doors, a **separate plaid** was worn, folded and belted about the body, ready to give protection against the elements when required. In modern times, this may also be worn with the kilt, when it is called a **belted plaid**, which can cause confusion.

As life in the Highlands became more settled, and there was less need to be out in all weathers and at night, the belted plaid lost its advantage, and the **kilt** (*Feile beag*) was the natural result, though not a simple one to achieve. The credit for the invention is usually given to an Englishman, Rawlinson by name, who had an ironworks in Lochaber—or in another version, at Tyndrum in Perthshire; we need not brand the story as a lie because two locations are given, Rawlinson may well have moved at some time—what is more important is that Rawlinson was friendly with Alasdair MacDonell of Glengarry and had available the services of a regimental tailor (named Parkinson, which is rather unfortunate as it has given chances for confusion). It is not very difficult to imagine these three heads being put together in an effort to devise an alternative to the belted plaid which would be more suitable to the changed times, and it is not beyond possibility that someone had already thought of tacking in the pleats of the plaid with the same object in view, so that all that would be left for Rawlinson and his friends was to tidy up the design and make it a practical proposition.

Whoever invented it, the type of short kilt that came into favour early in the eighteenth century was essentially what we have today.

There was a nineteenth-century vogue for box-pleats, which use less material than do knife-pleats and were consequently popular with the War Office, but that was a minor matter, and we have to concern ourselves more with the wearing of the kilt than with the making of it. People who should know better lay down many 'rules' for the wearing of Highland dress, forgetting that it is a dress like any other, and so is subject to variations of personal taste, and oblivious of the fact that there is no authority behind the rules. The length of the kilt is one thing that comes in for much regulation; one story has it that the bottom edge of the kilt should be level with the centre of the kneecap, another that it should be one inch (25 mm) off the floor when the wearer is kneeling upright, but either of these make the kilt far too long, so that it will saw the backs of the knees when it gets wet. The kilt should never hang lower than the top of the kneecap. Another old tailor's tale is that the kilt pin should be used to pin the upper apron to the lower; this will speedily result in a ripped kilt.

Our ancestors wore long shirts inside their kilts, plaids or trews; what they wore inside *those* was their own business, as it is ours today, but the kilt *was* a garment, not an over-garment. The jackets that they wore outside were often of tartan and cut to accommodate the bunching of the belted plaid, and so hung rather oddly to modern eyes, but otherwise they fell into line with current fashion and the owner's wealth or otherwise, and might at one time be plain and at another greatly enriched with fancy linings and slashed sleeves. Nowadays, at any rate for day wear, we tend to go in for jackets of light tweed or saxony in fairly plain patterns, and the most common styles are the Argyll pattern, with gauntlet cuffs and shoulder straps, and the plain 'sports jacket' type. A battledress blouse goes so well with the kilt that a day doublet, of tweed, is made on the same lines, though not at the same price. Whichever style is chosen for the jacket, it *must* be a proper kilt jacket. Few sights are more disturbing than that of an ordinary sports jacket worn with the kilt, unless it be a blazer, or a jacket belonging to a lounge suit; the decision as to which of these looks the worse is a difficult one. Raincoats and overcoats do not go particularly well with the kilt either, but may have to be worn for economic reasons; there is a type of waterproof cape worn by pipers which is quite

Figure 5

acceptable, but the ideal topcoat is a tweed Inverness cape.

Neckties in particular are a matter in which the personal conscience must guide. My own opinion is that the smaller and usually brighter pattern of a tartan tie can clash badly with the kilt, and that club and service ties are risky for the same reason. A tie which tones with the jacket is usually a much safer choice.

So far, I have concerned myself with everyday wear for men. The modern **Highland evening dress**, compounded of traditional elegance, military regulation and Victorian formality, is the peak of male finery and gives us every opportunity to outshine our partners while holding out to them the challenge and incentive to uphold Scotland's reputation for producing bonnie lassies.

The important things to be considered are the tartans to be avoided and the jackets to be worn, and the former need cause us very little trouble. The white-ground tartans, called 'Dress' tartans in the trade, are the descendants of the patterns formerly used for feminine wear and so are generally not suitable for men, although there are some exceptions; hunting tartans are also not the thing for dress wear.

Jackets are of many styles, from the Sheriffmuir, modelled on the old style worn with the belted plaid, through the semi-military doublets, which can be single- or double-breasted, and of waist-length or with short skirts, to simple designs after the style of the southern dinner jacket.

Figure 6

The choice is a personal one, and only the veriest hints can be given to guide it. The Sheriffmuir coat looks well and has tradition behind it, while the doublets are neat and smart and, if they did originally come from the Officers' Mess, are quite correct and suitable. The waist-length doublet, often called Montrose, has a tendency to ride up out of the belt; the longer type, in addition to being free of this trouble, can have pockets concealed in its tails, and this can be of great advantage to one unused to living in a sporran. In material, the choice is as wide as in

45

Figure 7 : the arisaid reconstructed

style; the Sheriffmuir coat looks particularly well in tartan, the doublets are usually in velvet and the dinner jacket in barathea, but there are still no rules beyond the dictates of personal taste and pocket, and it is up to the wearer to wear what he can carry best. A waistcoat can be worn with the open types of jacket, and this can be of tartan, can match the jacket, or can be of plain colour (but plain red is rather frowned upon in higher circles as having been the mark of the 'servant class'). For neckwear, a bow tie will usually be worn with an open type of jacket and a lace jabot with one that buttons up to the neck, but there are types of jacket that will suit either jabot or tie.

As with the Sassenach dark lounge suit, Highland day dress with a

46

dark jacket and plain tie will meet the needs of all the lesser degrees of formality, so it is generally not necessary to invest in a vast and expensive wardrobe.

When we come to trace the history of **women's dress**, we begin to run into trouble; it is logical to suppose that something analogous to the saffron shirt was worn, but there is nothing upon which we can base an opinion as to its appearance. Nor are we a lot better off when it comes to considering the **arisaid** (*Earrasaid*), which was the equivalent of the belted plaid in ladies' wear. There are some totally uninformative Victorian reconstructions by the artist McIan and quite a lot of airy writing, but all that really tells us anything is an account given by Martin Martin in his *Description of the Western Isles*, published in 1704. This at least makes it plain that the tartan was mainly white, with a few coloured lines, and that the garment reached from neck to heels; Martin goes on to say that it was fastened about the waist with a belt and pinned at the breast. This is not a promising foundation for a detailed picture, but provided the opportunity for some interesting experiments in which it was found that a double width of material, two to two and a half yards long (about two to two and a quarter metres) can be made into a garment on the lines of the belted plaid and in keeping with Martin's description. It has to be worn with the narrow way of the material round the body—that is, with the seam vertical— and is pleated and belted round the waist in the same manner as the plaid, although there are, of course, many fewer pleats. The loose material above the waist is then brought up under the arms and pinned at the front, leaving a considerable length hanging down behind; most of this is brought over the shoulders and fixed with the same pin as before, but enough remains hanging behind to serve as a hood in wet weather.

The arisaid might be worn over a full and heavy sleeved petticoat, but Martin says that sleeves of scarlet material were worn, ornamented with gold lace and plate buttons. The implication is that these were separate items, but it is probable that they were attached to some kind of short jacket or bodice.

Since the arisaid, female Highland fashion has tended to become simply whatever is the fashion of the day, either made in tartan or worn with a tartan sash, shawl or screen. An era of tartan gowns has passed us by and the current trend for female wear is towards the tartan skirt worn with a knitted jumper and tweed jacket. It can perhaps be said yet again that the full male kilt is not for the ladies; there are many styles of skirt, plain and pleated, that are more suited to the female figure and all look infinitely better than does the full kilt. A tartan cape or cloak is an efficient outer covering, directly in the tradition of the small plaid formerly worn out of doors.

For evening or other formal dress, a suitable frock is generally worn, with a tartan sash disposed in the manner approved by the Lord Lyon in accordance with the wearer's rank and station. The sash is worn diagonally round the body from hip to shoulder, either with the ends hanging down equally or with the longer end at the back. A clanswoman wears her sash pinned on the right shoulder and a chieftainess (this description includes the wife of a chief and the wife of a colonel of a Highland regiment) pins hers on the left; a woman who has married out of her clan wears her own tartan and pins her sash by its centre to the right shoulder and ties the ends in a large bow at the left hip. When it is necessary to keep the front of the dress clear, as for Scottish country dancing or when decorations are worn, a small loop at the centre of the sash fastens to a button at the back of the waist and the ends are pinned to the right shoulder and let fall down behind.

Influenced by the appalling spectacle of small girls capering through the Highland Fling decked out in the full panoply of a Victorian Highland chief, bodies such as the Scottish Official Board of Highland Dancing and the Committee of the Aboyne Gathering have, as is their right, devised and prescribed attractive and suitable dress for male and female dancers.

For male dancers, the Official Board lays down three styles of dress, corresponding to *a*, evening dress with Balmoral or Glengarry bonnet, a dirk and plaid being optional, *b*, day dress, and *c*, day dress without jacket and waistcoat, a white shirt and tartan or plain tie being worn. Black Highland dancing pumps are worn with all styles and the last mentioned is suitable also for competition country dancing.

Plate 1 : girl dancers in Aboyne dress

The Official Board's dress for female dancers is a kilt-style skirt worn with a white blouse that has either full- or half-length sleeves. A velvet jacket or sleeveless waistcoat may be worn if desired, as may a Balmoral-type bonnet to match the jacket, and there is a wide choice of hose; pumps are worn on the feet, and accessories in general are forbidden. The Aboyne dress (Plate 1, facing page 48) consists of a full skirt in tartan, white blouse, sleeveless velvet waistcoat, sash and pumps. This is also suitable for competition country dancing, but dance teams often wear white or light-coloured three-quarter length frocks and show tartan only in the sash. Among all this competition dancing, it must not be forgotten that people sometimes dance for pleasure, and for this the occasion governs the dress; one does not turn up at a Caledonian Ball in shirt-sleeve order on the strength of having to dance a Strathspey or two.

And now, a word about the accessories that form so large a part of Highland dress, noting in passing that the ladies again do not get much of a look in.

Lacking trouser pockets, the Highlander has instead his **sporran** (in English, a purse) which has descended, in both senses, from the simple bag, closed with draw-strings, that was attached to the belt of every medieval traveller; in due course this developed a fold-over top and, with the disappearance of the belted plaid, had to be slung on its own strap which now hung loose around the hips. From this came the modern hide sporran, with its tooled design on the flap and swinging tassels to the bag; these last are now more often than not entirely ornamental, but represent the strings that used to close the separate compartments in the main bag.

The skin of a small furry animal, if properly cured, can make a fine sporran, and it is not always necessary to commit murder to get suitable material. A friendly gamekeeper can often help, for he is sometimes obliged to do some trapping; he is also in a good position to come upon small beasties that have come to untimely ends. If the skin is simply sewn up into a bag, leaving the paws hanging and the head as a flap,

Plate 2: soldiers of the Scots Guards, piping and sword-dancing in the traditional military style

Figure 8

it will look very smart but the hair will quickly rub off the back. For this reason, a professionally made sporran will have a plain leather back; it may also have glass eyes and a plastic nose.

Another early design has the leather bag fitted to a metal top that opens like a purse and some examples exist in which a pistol is built into the top and a trick catch arranged to let it off if the release knobs are pressed in the wrong order. This is not a very effective anti-theft precaution, as the easiest way into a sporran is to cut the bag, and cannot have served any particularly useful purpose except that of frightening absent-minded owners.

A Victorian abomination of the metal-topped variety is the floor-sweeping horsehair sporran; now used, exclusively we must hope, by pipe bands and other military or quasi-military formations, the less said about it for general wear the better.

For dress wear, the sporran is almost always of sealskin and is silver-mounted; it may have either the purse type of top or a hinged flap overlaid with a metal fretted design, and will be worn on a strap and chain, instead of on the plain strap which is usual for day wear and better, because a chain worn regularly will soon damage the kilt.

If reports are true, the Highlander's footwear meant a good deal less to him than did the sporran which contained his immediate ration of

Figure 9

oatmeal, a sufficient reason for putting that item before shoes, hose and garters. The early Highlander, when he wore **shoes** at all, made them for the occasion by wrapping his feet in pieces of untanned deerskin and lacing these with thongs; he then cut drainage holes, so that the water which would be certain to get in, could get out again. These were called **brogain** (in English, brogues) but a short boot of calf-length made in a similar way was also worn, although it was said that a man who wore these had to get up an hour earlier than the man who wore brogues, because of the extra lacing. The Highland dancing pump is very much after the style of these brogues, although a lot neater, and so is the ghillie pattern of brogue for outdoor wear. Another type of outdoor shoe is the heavy hill shoe, with a forward-facing flap over the laces, but for everyday wear both for men and women, an ordinary stout brogue is fully satisfactory. Evening dress shoes for men are either lightweight or patent leather, ghillie type or strapped, and offer further opportunities for ornament with silver buckles; the ladies wear whatever evening shoes they wish.

The rule-makers tell us that shoes for wear with the kilt must be black, seemingly on the grounds that soldiers wear the kilt and soldiers wear black boots. The natural colour of leather, tanned or untanned, is brown, and this must have been the colour of the original brogues; depending upon which side of the skin was outside, they may even have been sueded. They would not have had inch-thick crepe-rubber soles, but would have lost nothing in appearance thereby. The colour of shoes is as free a choice as anything else about a Highland outfit; brown can go very well with a red or brown tartan, but black seems generally to suit a green one better.

Hose were formerly made from woven material, cut on the bias, tailored to the leg, and sewn up the back leaving a high-standing seam; this much we know, but there is more to it than that, and some very careful work is needed if the stocking is to be a good fit at the ankle and still be removable, for it has to stretch a lot to go over the heel. Until the secret is re-discovered, there is a fully adequate range of knitted hose to choose from; plain knitted for day wear and diced, or containing at least the elements of the tartan, for evening wear. The tops are either turn-down, or castellated in imitation of the old style. There is a legend that red and white diced hose are reserved for the military, but a record of the pattern dating from about 1800 makes no such suggestion, calling it just 'Hose, Old Pattern'.

Nowadays, stockings are generally kept up by an elastic **garter**, but a length of $1\frac{1}{4}$ in. wide webbing (30 mm) wound round the leg and tucked under itself is as efficient and more comfortable. In the days before turn-down tops, garters were tied with elaborate ornamental knots; if castellated-top hose are worn, these are still required, but it is difficult to get instruction in tying them. Some say that an ordinary tie knot will serve, others that it will not, and personal experiment is called for.

It may be of some comfort to know that the **sgian dubh** which is worn tucked into the stocking on the outside of whichever leg is the more convenient, is not classed as a weapon, at least to the extent that Members of Parliament who may appear in Highland dress are permitted to carry it into the House. The name means black knife, and one explanation of it is that the blade quickly becomes pitted and blackened by acid from the skin which impregnates the leather sheath. Another reason might be that it should be a *sgiath dubh*, a 'black wing', a name which could easily have been given to a knife which is known to have been carried as a secret weapon in an armpit sheath. Even if it did get its name by mistake, a black knife has to be black, and so a *sgian dubh* now has a black sheath and for most occasions a black haft as well; both are silver-mounted and jewelled to a degree varying with cost and use. Bone and horn are also used for hafts, and it was probably to these that the original blades made by the local smith were fitted; the semi-petrified wood found deep in the peat makes an exceptionally good haft, but this is not picked up every day and one suspects most *sgians* of being hafted either with plastic or with some imported hardwood.

If he had any wealth, the Highlander of old carried a good deal of it about with him in the form of ornaments to his dress. Members of a nation that cared little for money in the form of coin were deeply superstitious over having a proper burial should they die when away from home, and the weight of silver that was carried in the form of buttons, brooches and buckles was there for the purpose of dealing with this contingency after the owner had ceased to need them as ornaments. Nowadays, **buttons** for day wear are made of horn or leather and the belt, if worn, will probably have a brass **buckle**; silver does not go on show until the evening, except for the kilt pin and cap badge.

It seems probable that the **kilt pin** was originally used to hold the kilt up, and that it was moved to the bottom right-hand corner of the apron when the side straps were introduced for that purpose and Victorian notions of propriety demanded that the upper apron should be pinned to the lower; now that it has been realized that this is both unnecessary and damaging to the kilt, the pin is often worn higher up and has become, in any case, something of an optional extra, many people not wearing one at all. It is a harmless enough ornament though, and its small weight, worn low down, is enough to stop the apron flapping about when there is a bit of a breeze.

Brooches of various kinds and sizes figure in Highland dress for both men and women; the former having needed them mainly for anchoring the end of the belted plaid, it follows that the greater use is now by the ladies, in connection with their sashes. Traditional types of brooch are the ring-and-pin, in which a loop of material is pulled through the ring and the pin put through the loop without piercing the material, and the more familiar penannular type with its swivelling pin. Brooches were not always made of precious metals, and in fact brass was probably the most common metal used; whatever the material, embellishment with chased or engraved patterns was usual. No less traditional, but more concentrated upon in modern times, are the pierced Celtic designs with inset stones.

Deriving from the metal plate bearing a chief's crest and motto that used to be worn by his retainers, the clansman's **cap badge** now consists of a representation, in white metal or silver, of the crest encircled by a strap, buckled at the bottom and bearing the motto round it; the Chief's own badge dispenses with the buckle, which is the emblem of servitude and is therefore inappropriate to him. The badge is worn on the left side of the bonnet on a cockade made of ribbon, the colour of which proclaims the wearer's larger loyalties—white for Jacobite, black for the House of Hanover, and blue for Scotland.

Headgear is no more essential with the kilt than with any other dress, but if worn, it should preferably be neither a deerstalker hat nor a cloth cap; these, even in tartan, go badly with Highland dress. A beret may be regarded as acceptable, but the Balmoral type of bonnet comes nearest to tradition and suits either sex; the Glengarry bonnet is a more military style. Initially blue, either type of bonnet can have a diced band or border and the bobble, properly called a toorie, may be either red or blue; Balmorals can also be obtained in a variety of colours other than blue, but the brightly coloured, often tartan, knitted Tam-o'-Shanter is not male attire.

54

With the bonnet, fixed to it behind the badge, feathers are worn, the number of which denotes the rank of the wearer, three for a chief, two for a chieftain and one for a 'Highland gentleman'. We are told that these should be eagles' feathers, but others have doubtless served; as usual, the idea has been overdone, and one result is the military feather bonnet, in which the bonnet is entirely obscured by the feathers.

Traditional types of head-dresses for the womenfolk have almost entirely disappeared, surviving only in the **snood** worn with the Aboyne dance dress, which is no more than a length of ribbon which passes under the hair at the back of the head and is tied in a bow on top. The **mutch** was a frilled bonnet, decorated with lace and ribbon, and there was also the **kertch**, which is the subject of attractive but uninformative pictures and the usual vague descriptions. The general idea behind the kertch appears to have been a square piece of linen which was rolled diagonally, from one corner to the centre, the thick band thus formed being put round the head and pinned at the back and the rest of the material draping back to hang down behind.

Like tartan, Highland dress has suffered much from having been a subject for 'romance', and from writers who have been content to pass on earlier errors and obscurities. In these circumstances, it frequently becomes necessary to take a very careful look at things which have been accepted without question for too long, and to ask if they will really work. The result is frequently enlightening and always worthwhile.

Highland dress is in no sense a fancy dress. The wearer will find it suitable for most places and most occasions; and although the new-comer to the kilt will feel a bit strange at first, as well as perhaps having to overcome some prejudice in other people, neither will last long. It will only be a short while before you find that any strangeness comes with changing back into trousers.

HIGHLAND WEAPONS

Observers in the seventeenth and eighteenth centuries had quite a lot to say about the amount of armament carried by Highlanders of the clan era, even when they were going about ordinary peaceful business; little, if anything, needed to be added to make them ready for a full-scale war.

Undoubtedly the weapon that gave the clans their fighting power was the **basket-hilted broadsword**, miscalled the claymore (*Claidheamh mor*, a great sword). The true **claymore** was a heavy two-handed sword which might be up to about five feet (one and a half metres) in overall length, with which, in spite of the great weight of metal to be thrown about, it seems to have been possible to indulge in some quite energetic swordplay. The broadsword is a single-handed weapon, not only much lighter than the claymore, but so finely balanced as to feel almost weightless. Sir Walter Scott liked to use the name *Andrea Ferrara* for it, after a famous maker, and indeed, it seems that the blades at least were generally of continental manufacture. This was the weapon of the clan charge that no regular troops were able to withstand until Culloden; there, with artillery to sweep the field and the wind and sleet in the faces of the Jacobites, the regular soldiers of the Duke of Cumberland's army won the day, and thereafter the clans fought no more as clans.

In view of the length of time that has elapsed since the claymore was used in battle, the scarcity of iron that existed in the Highlands until quite recent times, and Acts of Parliament for disarming the clans passed after the Risings of 1715 and 1745, it must be held remarkable that many of either type of sword should have survived, but they have, and can be seen in plenty in museums all over Scotland, some merely as exhibits but others, like the Charmed Sword in the Clan Macpherson museum at Newtonmore, with stories attached. The Charmed Sword is a fine basket-hilted broadsword with the enviable reputation that no one bearing it has ever been wounded in an engagement. It originally belonged to one of the Duke of Argyll's men who objected to fighting against Bonnie Prince Charlie and therefore provided a substitute, as

Plate 3a:
MACLEOD OF HARRIS

This simple design, based upon the blue/black/green check, is a typical reversing pattern, pivoting around the red and yellow lines so that each half sett is the mirror image of those preceding and following it.

Plate 3b:
CAMPBELL OF ARGYLL

A tartan which would normally reverse can be made non-reversing by overchecking in alternating colours. There are many tartans of this kind, which is an intermediate type between the reversing and truly non-reversing.

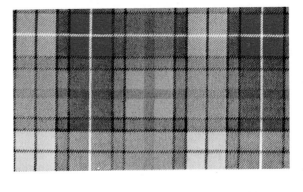

Plate 3c:
BUCHANAN

We owe this particularly clear example of a non-reversing pattern to an inaccurate artistic rendering, copied by manufacturers though a correct record was in fact available.

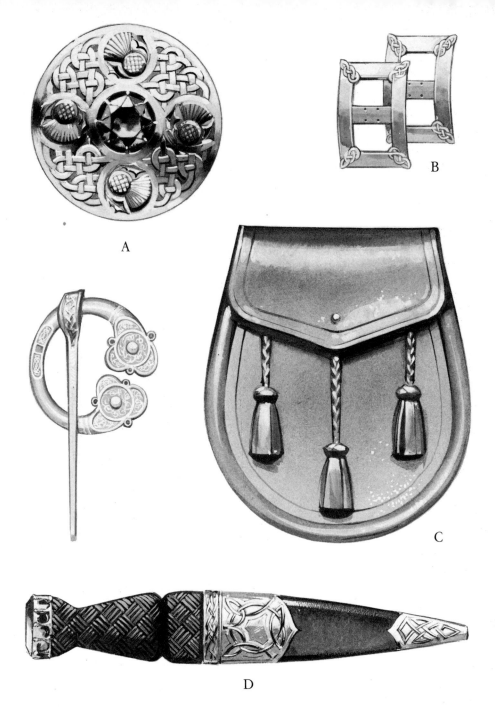

Plate 4a: *ACCESSORIES AND ORNAMENTS* (*1*) *A, plaid brooches; B, shoe buckles; C, a plain hide day sporran; D a* sgian dubh

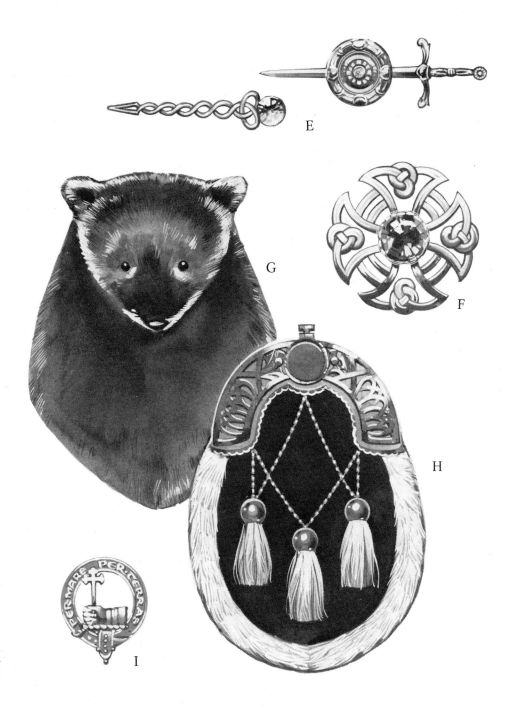

Plate 4b: ACCESSORIES AND ORNAMENTS (2) *E, kilt pins; F, plaid brooch; G, animal-head sporran; H, silver-mounted evening sporran; I, clan badge*

Plate 5a:
AN EIGHTEENTH CENTURY
UN-NAMED TARTAN
FROM SOUTH UIST

A modern copy of a tartan of the non-reversing type in which, in addition, the warp pattern differs from that of the weft. The original was in plain weave with red of a cherry shade.

Plate 5b: MACKINTOSH
This is a bold and simple tartan design which is of some antiquity. Its pair of broad green bars flanked by narrower blue ones provides the basis for upwards of a dozen red tartans from the Central Highlands.

Plate 5c: *designed in about 1907 for pipers of the 1st BATT., 1st GURKHA RIFLES, this dark tartan (miscalled Childers Universal) is also based upon Mackintosh, the red ground becoming black and the green and blue being rendered in two shades of green.*

could be done in those days; this substitute claimed the use of the sword, afterwards returning it to its owner, from whose descendants it came into the Cluny family. Duncan Macpherson, younger of Cluny, wore it during the Indian Mutiny when serving with the 42nd Royal Highland Regiment, the Black Watch. Plate 9, between pages 72 and 73, shows a tomb slab depiction of a claymore, a beautiful broadsword, and the Charmed Sword itself.

Giving rather longer range than either of the swords, the **Lochaber axe** was a variety of halberd; a long spike having on one side a broad axe head and on the other a hook, was fitted to a long shaft, and so gave the wielder a very useful extension to his reach. It is said to have been particularly useful against mounted adversaries, who could be dismounted with the hook and despatched with the axe, but no doubt there was more to it than that. Like the claymore and broadsword, the Lochaber axe has now become a ceremonial weapon, carried by City Guards and like bodies.

Protection was given against cut and thrust by the **targe** (*Targaid*), a round shield of wood covered with hide and strengthened with nails. The hide covering was usually tooled with an intricate design and the nails set out so as to be part of the pattern, thus producing such a work of art that enterprising craftsmen are now reproducing targes for use as ornaments. A targe would often have a socket set in the large central boss into which a spike could be fitted to give it some offensive value.

In battle, the targe was carried on a loop slipped over the forearm, so leaving the hand free to use the **dirk** (*Biodag*). This was a stabbing knife, with a thick blade about eighteen inches long (45 cm); the handle was gripped in the clenched fist, the direction of use being either forward and down or back and up, the latter being for the especial discomfiture of an enemy who thought he was creeping up undetected. The targe, free to swivel on its loop unless held close to the body, did not interfere with the operation of the dirk in this way. The dirk has now become a major ornament to ceremonial forms of Highland dress; both sheath and handle are heavily mounted with silver and cairngorms or other semi-precious stones, and the sheath is also contrived so as to carry a matching knife and fork.

Firearms were valued particularly for the chase, but no Highland gentleman could be counted dressed without his **pistols**, of which there were several famous makers whose products are now valuable collectors' pieces; Doune, in Perthshire, was formerly a great centre for pistol-makers. With the pistol, or other firearm, went the necessary **powder horn** and **shot pouch**. The long flintlock musket of the day was too cumbersome to be of much use in a Highland battle, where the method of attack was to discharge your pistols at the enemy and then throw them away before charging with broadsword, dirk and targe, for as the Highlanders said, if they won they would not need the pistols again, and if they had to run away they would not wish to be encumbered. With battle tactics like these, we can express no surprise that pistol-makers prospered. Downhill was, of course, the favoured direction for the charge, with the wind and the rain behind them as well, if it could be arranged, and we may be sure that in anything like a serious encounter a great deal of time would be spent in seeking a position from which the greatest advantage could be gained; the actual fight did not last long though, being decided more by the weight of the onslaught than the tenacity of the combatants.

Plate 6, facing page 64, shows a targe, a pistol, a dirk and two fine knives.

The **bow** lingered long in the Highlands, and its last authenticated use in battle was as late as 1644, at Tippermuir. Tradition puts the last use later still, in 1688 in a great battle between the MacDonalds and the Mackintoshes, but some doubt is felt about the accuracy of this; what we can expect is that the bow would remain in use as a hunting weapon for some time after it had become obsolete for war.

SCOTLAND'S TARTANS

AN INTRODUCTION TO TARTAN

To almost all non-Scots, and to many Scots as well, tartan is a matter of great fascination, a fascination that is unfortunately based in a large degree on myth and misapprehension which do a great deal to obscure the very real interest that the subject offers to the serious student.

Hazy memories of certain tartan patterns being appropriate to certain clans—almost always without any memory clear enough to reconstruct the pattern—were built upon by the romantic writers of the first half of the nineteenth century who constructed the great edifice of the Clan Tartan System, in which every clan had its own special tartan, which was, supposedly, regarded with an almost religious fervour. Tartan at this time being a large manufacture of the Scottish Lowlands, the people whose job it was to sell the cloth were by no means averse to such an idea, and a great proliferation of tartans resulted; tagging along at the end of it all came the necessity to prove one's right to a tartan by fair means or foul, culminating in the lists to be seen hanging up in the gift shops during the tourist season. Purporting to set out all rights in respect to tartan, these lists are usually given some such heading as 'Is your name here?' but might equally well be sub-titled 'If your name is not here, you have not got one.'

This attitude towards tartan has bred the idea that everything that there is to know about it is known already. This could hardly be further from the mark, for in reality very little indeed is known and a great deal is surmised, often on the basis of the weakest of evidence.

There is nothing so difficult to put right as a faulty tradition, and in the face of this tradition the early collectors of tartan failed when they elected to collect without investigating and to insist that any tartan worthy of the name must be called after some clan, family or district. While we have to be thankful to these first students of the subject for the survival of much that is of interest, their uncritical approach, except insofar as they generally seem to have regarded the other chap as being wrong, lost for them a chance to do important research work at a time much nearer to the events to which their studies related, and made the task of later workers more laborious.

Tartan traders must also bear some responsibility for perpetuating the myth, partly by keeping on telling the story or, at least, allowing customers to believe it, partly by the attitude that the people who sell tartan, and only they, know anything about it, and partly by the apparent fear that to tell a different story must have an adverse effect on sales.

Writers on the subject of tartan often appear to have formed their theories first and discarded any evidence that does not suit them, instead of assembling all the evidence and making a theory to fit it; it is not unknown for the same piece of evidence to be used to 'prove' completely opposite points, as occurred, for example, with the Culloden story instanced on page 69.

With all these hindrances to clear sight, it is hardly surprising that there is no general recognition of the fact that tartan is an absorbing subject for serious study, yet this is so, and once the bug has bitten the victim will be surprised to find in how many ways the study can be pursued. There is a wealth of documentary evidence awaiting analysis and an observant eye can discover specimens of tartan in the most unlikely places. In the Castle Museum at York, for example, there is a puppet dressed in a previously unknown tartan.

Proper study of tartan has much in common with archaeology and with detection. It can employ many skills, singly and collectively, and has a strong practical flavour, for it is often only possible to answer a question by putting oneself in the place of a Highland weaver of the sixteenth or seventeenth centuries and to do this at least a working knowledge of weaving is needed. The greatest merit of all is that anyone can join in, for the science is too young to have developed a closed shop approach.

WHAT IS TARTAN?

The word tartan is nowadays used to describe the pattern of the cloth, but this is a comparatively new meaning. Originally, it meant a type of cloth and had no reference to pattern; there are orders in existence (the Wilson letters—page 71) which date from near the middle of the nineteenth century and which make it clear that this meaning was still in use at that time, even though the more modern meaning had by then almost entirely supplanted it. One of those orders is quite clear, and asks for a supply of plain coloured tartan without any pattern, and the other is sufficiently ambiguous to cause the manufacturer to ask if a plain coloured cloth is intended, without expressing any surprise that this might be so.

The word is generally supposed to have been derived from the French *tiretaine* but there is an alternative view that it comes from the Gaelic *tarsuinn*, meaning 'across', in allusion to the weaving process; neither of these explanations is particularly satisfactory, for the meaning of *tiretaine* is obscure, and if the name comes from the Gaelic it seems very strange that the only Gaelic word for tartan is *breacan* which means 'speckled' or otherwise parti-coloured.

Tartan today signifies a cloth woven with coloured yarns in a regular pattern of lines and stripes which is the same in each direction of the cloth and generally, but not always, reverses about pivot lines in the pattern, so that each section of the design is the mirror image of the sections adjoining it; the comparatively rare exceptions to this rule are those in which the pattern repeats without reversing, but there is a compound type which has features of both types of design. Plate 3, facing page 56, illustrates these differences, and Plate 5, facing page 57, includes a tartan which is non-reversing both ways. The pattern is technically known as the 'sett'. Modern tartan may be woven in any type of textile and although wool is perhaps still most popular, silk and synthetics are much used.

The indigenous tartan of the Highlands in the years up to the Rising of 1745 was of the wool of the now-extinct Highland sheep, which gave a long and fine fleece particularly suitable for spinning into a fine hard

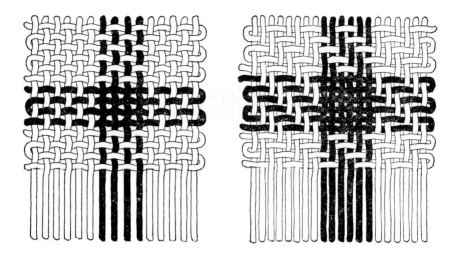

Figure 10: left, tabby weave; right, plain or 2/2 twill.

thread. The resultant cloth, woven in the staggered 'over two, under two' type of weave known as plain or 2/2 twill (as shown above, on the right), was also hard and fine, nearly weather-proof and very long-lasting, with a texture more like that of new linen than of a woollen fabric. Also shown in the diagram is the 'over one, under one' sequence of tabby weave.

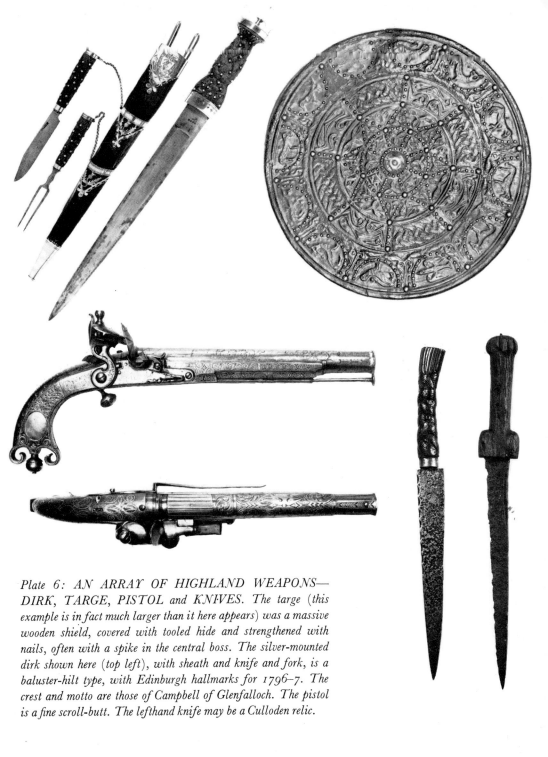

Plate 6: *AN ARRAY OF HIGHLAND WEAPONS—DIRK, TARGE, PISTOL and KNIVES. The targe (this example is in fact much larger than it here appears) was a massive wooden shield, covered with tooled hide and strengthened with nails, often with a spike in the central boss. The silver-mounted dirk shown here (top left), with sheath and knife and fork, is a baluster-hilt type, with Edinburgh hallmarks for 1796–7. The crest and motto are those of Campbell of Glenfalloch. The pistol is a fine scroll-butt. The lefthand knife may be a Culloden relic.*

THE EARLY HISTORY OF TARTAN...

From Roman records we know of the Celtic love of ornament and of their richly coloured cloaks, which Virgil described as 'striped and shining' (we must, however, remember that the Celts spread across a great swathe of north-west Europe, and that customs would have varied from tribe to tribe). In those days there was apparently no word with which to describe tartan as we know it today, and 'striped' may have been the nearest that writers could get to it; however, to assume that every time 'striped' (or something synonymous) is written, 'tartan' is meant, is quite unwarrantable, and so we cannot reasonably say that the Celtic Britons wore tartan.

In point of fact, the tartan type of pattern has much to recommend it to a comparatively primitive weaver. It is simple to weave and, being a balanced cloth, the warp and weft threads can be of the same gauge and substance. Its exuberant colour effect is achieved by the inter-weaving of bands of different colours—each colour in a tartan mixes equally with every other colour and with itself—and each colour appears in relatively small areas, thus overcoming the greatest problem of the dyer, that of making successive batches of dyeing to match accurately. Last, and perhaps most important in our present context, the tartan pattern is of the abstract repetitive type that is the basis of all Celtic art. Thus we are free to surmise that our Celtic forebears wore some kind of tartan patterned cloth, so long as we do not regard this as being proved.

References in similar terms to those used by Virgil occur down the years: the Bishop of St. Andrews writes to Malcolm III in the late eleventh century concerning clothes of 'divers colours' and several Church ordinances of the thirteenth century mention striped clothing.

Plate 7: George IV in Highland dress, portrayed by David Wilkie. The King's ceremonial visit to Edinburgh in 1822, a generation after the lifting of the ban on Highland dress which had been imposed after Culloden, caused an explosion of interest in tartan and a rush to don 'Highland garb' in the 'right' clan tartan. (Reproduced by gracious permission of H.M. The Queen)

In the middle of the fourteenth century, the accounts of John, Lord of the isles, note the purchase of *braccatarum de tiretatana*, ingeniously translated as 'tartan trews', but we have to wait until 1538 for the first unequivocal mention of tartan, when among other items of material for kingly garments, there was purchased three ells of 'Heland tertane, to be hoiss for the Kingis Grace', James V. Even now, we are not told anything about the pattern of the tartan, although Lord Archibald Campbell announced that it would have been of the 'brilliant Royal tartan'—which was almost certainly unknown at that time and for about two hundred years after, its first recorded appearance being in Wilson's Pattern Book in 1819. More likely than any other pattern would be a simple two-colour check such as that now called Rob Roy, which was overwhelmingly popular for trews over a long period.

From this time on, although we are still told nothing about the pattern of the cloth worn by the Highlanders, it becomes more evident that something resembling our modern tartan had developed. 'Light coverings of wool of many colours', reported by the French historian Beaugué to have been worn by Highlanders at the siege of Haddington in 1548, sounds suspiciously like modern tartan, and the frequently reproduced 1631 woodcut showing Highlanders in the army of Gustavus Adolphus gives a very clear picture of the tartan of their dress, even though the garments are not the conventional idea of Highland dress—excepting one, which is a very much more accurate picture of the belted plaid than many a modern artist has managed.

From early in the eighteenth century, portraits of clan chiefs and other notables show that by that time tartan in its present form had emerged, although existing portraits are unanimous in that they show no tartan we now know as a 'clan tartan'. This fact has occasioned some comment, it being argued that a chief would surely wear his clan tartan when having his portrait painted; since he did not, there were 'obviously' no clan tartans at that time. I feel myself that even if we can assume that each artist was photographically accurate, the only proof implicit in the portraits is that the chief, unlike his clansmen, was not restricted to wearing whatever ordinary run-of-the-mill pattern the local weaver turned out. There is also a persistent tale that the artist Richard Waitt took horse-loads of canvases around, ready painted except for the face; this does not in itself prove that there were no clan tartans in existence, but only that if there were, people did not bother much about them.

It is difficult to know where or when the idea that every clan had its own tartan found its beginning. An epic poem, the *Grameid*, written in Latin in 1691, tells of Dundee's campaigns in support of the Stuarts and seems to make it clear that the various regiments wore uniform patterns of clothing, but it would be reasonable to expect that the regiments would be kitted out by their chiefs, who would naturally order large quantities of cloth of one pattern. At the beginning of the eighteenth century, the chiefs of Clan Grant upon two occasions ordered that their men should turn out in uniform tartans, and gave a rough idea of the pattern—'Red and greine set dyce all broad springed'—but the very need to give such orders suggests that uniform tartans were by no means usual wear. In fact the nearest approach to uniformity is reported by Martin Martin in his *Description of the Western Isles of Scotland*, first published in 1703 and reprinted 'very much corrected' in 1716. Martin has a great deal to say that is of interest to the student of tartan and which is meaningful if no attempt is made to read into it what is not there. In connection with the patterns of the tartans of his day, Martin said:

'Every Isle differs from each other in their Fancy of making Plads, as to the Stripes in Breadth, and Colours. This Humour is as different thro the main Land of the Highlands, in-so-far that they who have seen those Places are able, at the first View of a Man's Plad, to guess the Place of his Residence.'

He probably meant just that, and not that there was in existence in 1703 a rigidly defined system of district tartans as has been assumed by some.

Perhaps the first voluntary use of tartan as a uniform was among those protesters against the 1707 Act of Union, but this was in the Lowlands; the Highlands cared little for what might happen in Parliament, either in Edinburgh or London. Yet it seems certain that by the time of the Jacobite Rising in 1745, some idea of uniform clan tartans had grown up, to survive the period following the '45, when tartan was forbidden to the Highlanders at home, and grow into the rigid Clan Tartan System that reached its peak in mid-Victorian times.

Romance is notorious for building lofty structures upon little or no foundation and it is probable that the whole clan tartan edifice rests upon the economic circumstances of the day. Nothing is less likely than that the weaving of tartan was done by the women of the clan, except in isolated cases when a laird's wife or daughter might apply herself to the art. Most of the women were far too busy with their domestic chores and weaving is a full-time skilled trade such as is best pursued by a specialist. Once such a specialist had set up in business in a village, he was blessed with a captive clientele which made it unnecessary for him to produce a large range of patterns; the smaller the range the better, so far as he was concerned, for fewer patterns mean fewer problems with stocks of yarn in different colours and, since the major work in handweaving is in setting up the loom, one long length is better than several short ones. In a Highland village of the early eighteenth century, it might be surprising if all the people were *not* wearing the same, or recognizably similar, tartans, but it must be emphasized that this was unlikely to have been because they were so proud of it that they would wear no other; more likely, they complained bitterly about the weaver's unwillingness to give them any other except at a much higher price. Chiefs, of course, would be able to afford or command whatever pattern they might desire.

There is good probability that many talents were involved in the production of early eighteenth century Highland tartan. The wool would certainly have been spun by the women as they went about their daily tasks, using the spindle for the purpose, for the spinning wheel was a latecomer to the Highlands; very likely the children had the job of gathering the plants that were used to dye the spun yarn, and another job likely to fall to the womenfolk, as sub-contractors, was that of making up the 'warp', the lengthwise threads of the cloth made up into a bundle for winding on to the loom.

In this connection, Martin tells us:

'The Women are at great pains, first to give an exact Pattern of the Plad upon a small rod, having the number of every Thred of the Stripe upon it.'

Presumably dissatisfied with the meaning of this, in the second edition

68

he altered 'small rod' to 'piece of wood', without making the meaning any clearer, but later authors took up the statement and declared that it meant that a woman who wanted a piece of plaiding took to the weaver a strip of wood around which were wound coloured threads, with the proper number of turns for each stripe in its right order. Why she should have done this instead of taking a piece of the cloth to the weaver is not explained, and the whole idea has a rather mythical look about it, especially as none of these pattern sticks has survived, although there are several people who know somebody whose grandmother had one.

There are so many good reasons why such things would be valueless to a weaver that it is extremely difficult to believe that they ever really existed, and the only likely interpretation of Martin's remark is that the women made the warps for the weaver by winding yarn around pegs set in the side of the house, or in the ground, and when it was complete, wound the whole bundle, figure-of-eight fashion, round either a 'small rod' or a 'piece of wood' to make it easy to carry to the weaver.

The Jacobite Rising of 1745 added its own quota of inconclusive evidence about the use or otherwise of clan tartans.

An account by an officer of the Jacobite army contains the remark:

'We M'Donalds were much perplex'd, in the event of ane ingagement, how to distinguish ourselves from our friends and nighbours the M'Donalds of Sky, seeing we were both Highlanders and both wore heather in our bonnets, only our white cockades made some distinction.'

As the MacDonalds of Skye were on the Hanoverian side, this was a valid point from which one author drew the inference that the Mac-Donalds had a common clan tartan and another that they did not, for if they had, it would have been mentioned. Such are the pitfalls waiting for those who try to prove where no proof exists!

A very well-known painting, executed by David Morier shortly after the collapse of the Rising, purports to show an incident at the Battle of Culloden. Well drawn by an artist of high repute, the painting shows a group of Highland rabble being beaten back by well-turned-out Hanoverian troops acting with parade-ground precision; the seven

Highland figures shown are wearing between them twenty-two different tartans, none of which corresponds to any modern clan tartan. Even allowing for the fact that we can never expect anything like photographic accuracy from a manual artist, this takes a bit of swallowing, and the reason behind it is unlikely to be a simple and straightforward one.

It has been repeated from book to book that the models for the Highlanders in the picture were believed to be actual prisoners taken at Culloden, and if this is true we know that prisoners were stripped of their clothing when they were taken and can surmise that they were in no position to argue about what tartan was given them to wear. However, the statement about prisoners being used seems to be directly traceable to Lord Archibald Campbell, who seems to have relied heavily on his sense of intuition, and who claims only that they *must* have been Highland prisoners, for no others could wear Highland dress properly! If the models were not Highlanders, as now seems more likely than before, the pattern of their tartans would have no significance for them. So does another contentious point become meaningless.

In 1746, as part of the repressive measures to keep the Highlands under control, the Government of Great Britain passed an Act forbidding the wearing of tartan and Highland dress by any other than Highland soldiers of the British army; cloth that was no longer wanted was no longer made, and so, except for a few isolated fragments of cloth, all connected in some way with the Rising, we have no positive knowledge of pre-1745 tartan patterns beyond what can be gleaned from paintings. This was the end of a chapter, and when the proscription of Highland dress was raised a different set of circumstances altogether prevailed.

The provisions of the Act of 1746—familiarly known as the Dress Act—were in force from 1747 to 1782, and when the sun again rose on tartan it revealed a very different scene from that of earlier days.

For thirty-five years, tartan had been forbidden to the Highlander at home, but it had been used as a recruiting inducement for the Army —in 1745 there were two Highland Regiments and in 1782 there were ten, while nine more had been raised and disbanded during this period —and a great demand for the cloth had arisen in the New World colonies, where emigrant Highlanders could still wear it and it also provided a cheap and durable clothing for their slaves.

Because of all this, tartan had ceased to be an industry carried on by isolated weavers in their villages and become instead a large-scale Lowland industry, turning out cloth in great quantities for the Government and for export. Our knowledge of this period is much more complete, almost entirely owing to the activities of one firm; indeed, so dependent are we upon them that we have constantly to remind ourselves that there were others who may have thought differently and to take care not to allow a monopoly of history to this one.

The firm of William Wilson and Son, of Bannockburn, seems to have originated with William's father rather before the middle of the eighteenth century and continued to weave tartans until 1907; the whole business then went over to what had been a subsidiary activity, making carpets, and the firm passed out of existence in 1924.

It is evident that some early Wilson had an eye for posterity, for enormous quantities of the firm's records were preserved for later study. Something like twelve thousand letters and orders, dating back to 1792, are known to exist and from these alone it is no difficult matter to trace the growth of trade and the proliferation of patterns during these formative years of the tartan trade. Some of the letters contain information about patterns not otherwise recorded and many have fragments of the actual material, sent in as patterns, attached to them; these fragments are generally well-preserved and give a very good impression

71

of what the colours of old tartans really were. This treasure-house is supplemented by the Key Pattern Book that Wilsons compiled in 1819, when the boom had begun and the need for firm records of all the patterns that they made became necessary to the efficiency of their business. As the boom continued, more pattern books were compiled, and copies of them have survived to help tell the story of the later years of the tartan age.

As might be expected, the raising of the ban brought no instant rush of orders from the Highlands. Most of the earliest of the patterns are fancy ones made in narrow widths for plaiding and given names that might be expected to appeal to the Highlander far from home, such as Aberdeen, Dundee, New Bruce, Old Bruce and so on; even at this stage, though, there were Gordon Sett, Robertson Sett and Stewart's Sett to give a general indication that the clan tartan idea was alive at the end of the eighteenth century.

From 1800 to 1822 there was a steady proliferation of patterns as the Clan Tartan idea took slow but increasing hold and the demand for these and for purely ornamental patterns began to build up in the Highlands. The Key Pattern Book contains, in round figures, thread counts for two hundred tartans (sample thread counts are given in the Appendix on pages 111–16), with full weaving data, of which about half are named tartans, the rest being equally divided between tartan patterns known only by numbers and small check patterns of general utility; about one-third of the named tartans have clan names, the rest being either clearly named after some person or place—Aberdeen, The Marchioness of Huntly's Tartan, Caledonian Sett, and so on—or possibly named after the place where a piece of the old tartan of the pattern was discovered—Lochaber, Lochiel Tartan—or given some topical name such as Wellington, Waterloo or Regent. One design was made by William Wilson upon his marriage in 1775 and named after his wife, Janet Wilson Sett; alas, this marriage tribute is now *The* Wilson Tartan!

At this time, Highland chiefs knew little about what tartans might be reckoned to be appropriate to their clans. In 1817, Duncan MacPherson of Cluny certified as the tartan of his clan a Wilson design with the imposing title of 'No. 43, or Kidd Sett, or Caledonia Pattern', in spite

Plate 8a: MURRAY OF ATHOLL
Correspondence with Stewart of Garth
dating from 1815 records that Robertson of Struan had tried, some thirty
years earlier, to establish the correct
pattern of the Robertson tartan; fail-
ing, he adopted this, then called simply
Atholl Sett.

*Plate 8b: in spite of Struan's lack of
success (see above), this, the ROB-
ERTSON tartan, was being made in
the Lowlands under that name at that
time. It follows the pattern of a coat
worn by Prince Charles Edward at a
ball in 1745.*

*Plate 8c: this pattern was in Wilsons of
Bannockburn's 1819 list under the name
MACPHERSON OF CLUNY'S
TARTAN; but Cluny had, in
1817, certified as the tartan of his clan
a Wilson design named 'No. 43, or
Kidd Sett or Caledonia Pattern', a
fancy pattern loosely related to Royal
Stewart, (see also Plate 12).*

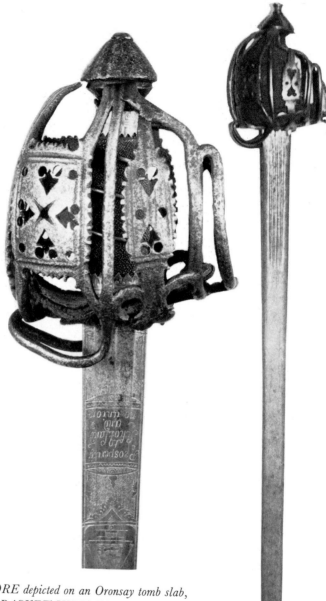

Plate 9: a sheathed CLAYMORE depicted on an Oronsay tomb slab,
dated 1539 (above left); a BASKET-HILT BROADSWORD
dating from about 1715, with a Jacobite inscription on the blade – on the
facing side, a figure of St Andrew and the words 'Prosperity to Schotland
and No Union' and on the hidden side, 'For God, My Country, and
King James the 8'; and (right), THE CHARM SWORD OF THE
MACPHERSONS, a basket-hilt Andrea Ferrara with cross mark and
circle – traditionally no one wearing it has ever been wounded.

Plate 10: an eighteenth century print (facing page)

The Scottish Highlander.   Un Montagnard d'Écosse.

This Plate is most Humbly Inscribed to the Right Honourable the Lord Temple
by his Lordships most Obedient Humble Servant Wm Moser.

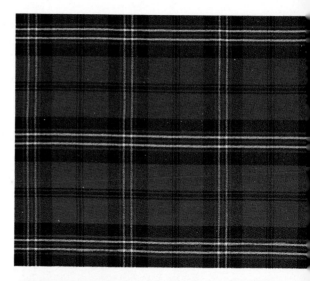

Plate 11 : the SCOTT tartan is one of about 75 whose origin can be traced only to the Vestiarium Scoticum *of 1842 and the supporting Cromarty Ms of about 20 years earlier. The similarity to McGregor is perhaps not coincidental.*

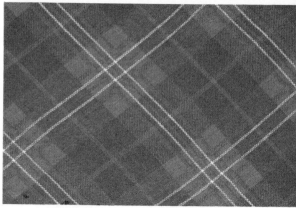

Hunting tartans, engendered by a supposed tradition of 'camouflage', are made by weaving the pattern of a bright clan tartan on a dark ground. This is HUNTING SCOTT, *in ancient colours.*

Dress tartans, made by weaving the clan tartan on a light ground, are natural descendents of the arisaid setts formerly worn by women. This is DRESS SCOTT, *here shown in modern colours.*

of there being also on Wilsons' books a 'MacPherson of Cluny's Tartan' (Plate 8, facing page 72), the name of which shows that it had a good claim, even if we do not know which MacPherson of Cluny wore it; in 1818, Patrick Grant of Redcastle bought two hundred yards (a hundred and eighty metres) of 'New Bruce' to be the tartan of his clan. Even before this, in 1815, General David Stewart of Garth, the well-known historian of the Highlands, was carrying on a lengthy correspondence with Alexander Robertson of Struan, concerning the possibility of preserving specimens of the old Clan tartans, from which the most significant fact to emerge was that several old men of the Robertson clan, reckoned to be versed in such things, had been unable to agree on what the Robertson tartan had looked like in its pre-1745 form. (The Robertson tartan now worn is shown in Plate 8, facing page 72.) Struan thereupon adopted the Atholl tartan—which is now called only Murray of Atholl (Plate 8, facing page 72)—but Wilsons *had* a 'Robertson' tartan at this time and a precious relic belonging to the Robertsons is a waistcoat (of the same pattern) worn by Prince Charles Edward at a ball during his 1745 campaign.

With all this confusion in the minds of those who should have known, it cannot be counted surprising that we, some hundred and fifty years later, have sometimes to ask ourselves where all the clan tartans came from in the first place. The easy answer is that when MacBloggs wanted a tartan for his clan he went along to the nearest tartan merchant, who produced a little book in which it was laid down that there was once a Donald Stewart who, from having received less than his proper portion of something, was known as *Dhomnuill a'Blaigh*—Donald of the small part—from whom all the MacBlaighs (and hence the MacBloggs) are descended, and so the MacBloggs were a sept of the Stewarts and 'entitled' to the Stewart tartan. Or our MacBloggs might have had to tour the tartan shops, until he found one that saw in him a heaven-sent chance to unload a line that was not selling very well, in the fairly certain knowledge that MacBloggs did not know what his tartan looked like anyway.

But this is the *easy* answer to the problem, and easy answers to complex questions are seldom the right ones. I have no doubt that what has been outlined did occur, and we know that a clan tartan could be chosen from a manufacturer's book of patterns if such were desired, but it seems hardly believable that nothing at all survived in the way of pre-1745 specimens of everyday tartans to be found and copied by the commercial weavers. George Hunter, an army clothier, toured the Highlands between 1820 and 1822 in search of old patterns and it is unlikely that Wilsons would not have taken steps at an even earlier date, for they were astute business men who worked hard at their trade, and the Wilson sons travelled many miles as sales representatives for the firm.

By 1822, the idea of clan tartans was at least established and the stage was set for the next act.

Admirably stage-managed by Sir Walter Scott and General Stewart of Garth, the visit to Edinburgh of George IV in 1822 was the occasion of a great tartan explosion and of a rush to get clan tartans, even when these had not previously been known, to wear at the various functions that took place. Plate 7, facing page 65, shows the King in all his Scottish finery. Thus was the tartan business set on the crest of the wave which still rolls on.

With the belief in, and demand for, clan tartans well established, there naturally followed lay interest in them, running alongside a general interest in the Highlands, which romantic writings had transformed, in the mind of every man, from a country of the lowest savages to one inhabited only by the highest kind of hero. Garth had recently published his *Sketches of the Character, Manners and Present State of the Highlanders of Scotland* and this was followed in 1831 by James Logan's *The Scottish Gael*. Both these set out to extol the virtues of the Highlander to the exclusion of any faults. Logan's book is chiefly remarkable for its having been the first attempt by anyone to convey the detail of a tartan pattern to the reader. This was done in tabular form, giving the colours of the stripes in order and stating the width in units of an eighth of an inch (3 mm approximately), '2' signifying $\frac{1}{4}$ in., '$\frac{1}{2}$' meaning 1/16 in. and so on. It is unfortunate that Logan chose to use measurements, rather than threads, of each colour, because the pitch of the threads (that is, the number to a fixed distance) is liable to vary between warp and weft (in order to square up the pattern) and even from place to place along the length of the cloth, but he left the germ of an idea for others to work

74

on and gave us a fairly accurate account of nearly fifty clan tartans of his day.

However, by far the most important contribution to the tartan lore of this period was a compendious volume entitled *Vestiarium Scoticum: from the Manuscript formerly in the Library of the Scots College at Douay. With an Introduction and Notes by John Sobieski Stuart*. This was published in 1842, although the preparatory work was in hand in 1829, and was the work of two brothers, John who contributed the text and Charles who provided the illustrations; it was the first book to contain facsimile plates of tartans. The brothers, originally named Allen,* were widely supposed to be grandsons of Prince Charles Edward and about 1828 they were claiming to have in their possession some ancient manuscripts containing details of the old clan tartans. There were three of these manuscripts, the earliest having been discovered at the Scots College at Douai, another, identical in all essentials, found in the St. Augustine Monastery at Cadiz, and a third, a 'late and inferior copy' of the others, obtained from an Edinburgh street porter. Only the last of these, which remains extant, has been seen by any eyes other than those of the brothers themselves, and the whole business has been shown quite conclusively (by D. C. Stewart and J. C. Thompson) to be a clumsy hoax, but at the time the Highland world was hungry for tartan and belief in the brothers was sufficient to ensure acceptance of their pronouncements, and so seventy-five, or thereabouts, of our most respected clan tartans are blatant forgeries. However, not everybody was willing to accept the brothers' stories; Sir Walter Scott who, despite his excursions into romance, knew a thing or two, was highly suspicious and in particular would have nothing to do with the idea of Lowland tartans, a number of which are included in manuscript and book. Between Sir Walter and Sir Thomas Dick Lauder who did accept the brothers' claims, there is voluminous correspondence and it is evident that Sir Thomas was thought to be worth cultivating, for he was allowed to make a copy of the manuscript which 'Mr Charles Stuart Hay, with very great politeness, agreed to illuminate for me with drawings of all the Tartans'. Sir Thomas's copy of the document, with drawings by Charles Sobieski,

* They also used the names Hay Allan and Stuart Hay.

was presented to Queen Mary by his grand-daughter, and now resides in the Royal Library at Windsor Castle. While the list of the tartans that it contains differs somewhat from that of the published *Vestiarium Scoticum*, both contain the Rothesay tartan, with almost identical descriptions and totally different illustrations.

To analyse in detail the weaknesses of the *Vestiarium Scoticum* would be to take more space than is available and to steal someone else's thunder. It is sufficient to say that as the original documents contained no illustrations nor any measurements, the means of reconstructing a pattern is absent, and so any reconstruction must be the product of the brothers' own imaginations. 'Clann-Lewid' (that is, MacLeod) 'hath thre blak stryppis upon an zellow fylde and in ye myddest of ye zallo sett ane stryp of twal threiddis scarlatt' is typical of a *Vestiarium Scoticum* description and cannot possibly have any firm meaning when taken on its own.

When popularization of the Highlands set in during the reign of Queen Victoria, tartans took a new turn. Now it was no longer just a matter of a tartan for everybody, there had to be a tartan for every occasion as well: clan tartan for everyday wear, hunting tartan for the hill, dress tartan for the evening and the ballroom (Plate 11 facing page 73, shows the Scott clan, hunting and dress tartans), and even in some cases funeral tartans; all this was a far cry from the wardrobe of the clansman of the previous century which it tried to imitate, but quite in accord with the Victorian tendency to overdo things. When colours became so improved that they were too strident for use on the hill, the clan tartan was made upon a dark ground of green, brown or blue in place of red. The old colours, obtained from infusions of local plants, had been bright enough, but they were subdued, and because the colours blended well, the brightest of tartans had a softness that made them not out of place in the field; the earliest synthetic dyes, and many later ones too, on the other hand, introduced a harshness that can be painful to the eyes. It is to the Victorian 'improvers' that we owe the very dark greens and almost black blues of many modern tartans, shades that no Highland dyer would have attempted, for he wanted his colours to be distinguishable from each other, so that the pattern could be seen.

76

The women of the Highland clans never wore clan tartans; theirs were usually white, with an open design of coloured bands (Plate 20 facing page 97), and may even have been, in the first instances, blankets caught up in haste and wrapped around the body for outdoor protection. The white-grounded tartans called 'dress' are therefore developments of the women's dress, and although they are widely used for men's evening wear the use is a mistaken one, based on a confusion of the meanings of the word 'dress'.

The use of funeral setts, except by the over-romantic and over-rich, must be regarded as a long stretch of the imagination, although there are many such setts about. In broad outline, they take the form of a clan tartan rendered in black and white and so are only applicable to simple patterns.

The Victorian era fixed the Clan Tartan idea in men's minds and converted all the myths into inviolable truths; henceforth it was not possible to disagree with anybody about anything connected with tartan, except acrimoniously.

But there *were* people concerned with keeping the record straight and in 1850 Thomas Smibert published *The Clans of the Highlands of Scotland*, while the brothers William and Andrew Smith, of Mauchline, produced *Authenticated Tartans of the Clans and Families of Scotland*, both with the aim of putting on record the proper tartans of the various clans. It is evident that a good deal of careful research went into both these books, although Smibert warns against putting too much faith in what the chiefs had to say on the subject.

The Smith brothers were makers of snuff boxes and similar knick-knacks which were 'finished' with pictures which were stuck on and varnished. For the making of tartan patterns for covering the boxes, they invented a most ingenious machine that ruled rows of parallel lines in opaque ink, first across the paper and then at right angles. Black paper was used and the colours were ruled in ascending order of darkness beginning with the lightest, and the result was a quite remarkably realistic representation of a plain-weave cloth. This machine made the plates for *Vestiarium Scoticum* and for the Smiths' own book, but was soon ousted by lithography as a printing process.

As the Lowland tartan industry grew up, its products found their

77

way to England as well as the more far-flung outposts already mentioned, and achieved such popularity that local industries grew up to make the material for home consumption and in competition with the Scots. One such centre of the English tartan weaving business was at Norwich where a great deal of worsted weaving was carried on and the Norwich weavers became quite dangerous competitors of Wilson & Son, one of whose customers is on record as complaining that the Norwich weavers charged only one penny for the same amount of red in a tartan as Wilsons charged sixpence for.

Some of the Norwich work was no more than copying Wilson's products, often not very well, but Norwich was noted for its woollen shawls and a collection of strips of material from one firm shows not only high-class work but some interesting developments of the tartan idea in their patterns; some are simple tartans, others are tartans with the warp stripes different from those of the weft, and in a third type the warp and weft patterns are the same, but in different colours.

All this has passed away now, apparently because when the hand loom was superseded by the power loom, Norwich had neither water power to drive the machinery nor coal to make steam to provide the power. But the Norwich museums have a good collection of old textile machinery and of samples of material made with it.

To the research worker, the message of Norwich is clear. It is to seek tartan where it is least likely to be found, for the likely places have already been worked out.

By the end of the nineteenth century, tartan might be said to have stabilized. The setts were there in all their gaudy profusion, all the myths and untruths were believed in implicitly and long lines of grandmothers were invoked to prove rights to tartans; in 1886 there had appeared the forerunner of the modern tartan 'picture-book', James Grant's *The Tartans of the Clans of Scotland* showing seventy-two tartans in the now-standard arrangement that gives a short history of each clan and a picture of its tartan.

It might be thought that there was nothing more to be said, but tartan is a live business, as it has always been, and does not stand still, so something had to happen—which it did, although we had to wait a while.

About the end of the First World War, somebody got the idea of using soft pastel shades of colour to replace the ordinary colours of tartan which had by then become unbearably vivid and harsh; these were called 'ancient' colours, which immediately led to tartans woven in them being called 'ancient' tartans, though they were identical with those made in the earlier shades, now called 'modern'. Naturally 'ancient' tartans began to sell better than 'modern' ones, and the less scrupulous dealers allowed the customer to think that they *were* ancient designs for that very reason, so a situation of great confusion grew up, not eased at all by the fact that some tartans, such as Old Stewart and Old Munro, contain the word 'old' as part of their just title, no matter what colours are used to weave them. These ancient colours are supposed to represent the colours obtained from the old natural dyestuffs, and one has occasionally heard a shopkeeper blandly informing a customer that the tartans are in fact vegetable-dyed; this however, is most unlikely to be true of a mass-produced tartan, although some vegetable-dyed tweeds can be had without too much difficulty.

Another, more recent development in the colour of tartans has been the invention of 'reproduction' colours, which are also sometimes called 'muted'. Although there have been many copies, the original range was based on a piece of tartan dug up by a peat-cutter on

Culloden Moor in 1946. Probably a relic of the battle, the colours of this fragment were very much what one might expect of a piece of tartan buried in peat for two hundred years, dull, with warm black for true black and olive brown for green. Reproduction tartans can look very nice, but it is the colours that are 'reproduction', the pattern is the same as any other.

It cannot be emphasized too strongly that in speaking of tartan it is the pattern, technically known as the sett, that governs what we call it. A given sett, woven in 'modern', 'ancient' and 'reproduction' colours will look very different, but it will be the same tartan. Plate 12 shown opposite illustrates this point.

As normal development, tartan patterns have continued to increase in number. Apart from the steady demand for more clan and family tartans, new 'fancy' patterns have made their appearance and there was a few years ago a spate of designs from Canada, where several new 'province' setts have been designed.

A modern tendency is for an element of pseudo-heraldry to creep into the choice of colours for a tartan; instead of a design being executed as an attractive pattern, 'purple for the heather', 'blue for the mountains', 'silver for the river' are worked in, a principle quite foreign to traditional tartan design, in which colour and pattern were completely abstract. Another way in which several established tartans have suffered of late is for the sett to be left recognizable but the colours entirely changed from the original, to make a 'new' pattern.

The total number of tartans now recorded is probably in excess of a thousand, many of which are manufacturers' 'fancy' patterns that have never been taken up as clan tartans, so the need for jiggery-pokery of this kind is difficult to see. In any case, the chap who designed the tartan the first time usually made the best arrangement of pattern and colour, so meddling with a design seldom improves it. Chunkier colours and clearer identification were characteristic of the old patterns, modern tartans being spindlier with a greater shading of colours, following on from the efforts of the Victorian improvers who deliberately made fine lines finer and so on.

The most significant developments in the modern history of tartan are in the paperwork rather than in the cloth. Those with suitable

Plate 12: the red Clan tartan of the MACPHERSONS was certified by the Chief in 1817. The colours shown here approximate closely to those then in use. (See also Plate 8.)

The same tartan in 'ancient' colours, developed to counter the harshness of early synthetic dyes. In such cases, 'old' and 'ancient' refer only to the colours, not the design.

'Reproduction' colours were developed after the Second World War, when a peat cutter on Culloden Moor found a fragment of tartan thought to have lain there since the battle.

Plate 13: in 1848 Queen Victoria and the Prince Consort paid their first visit to Balmoral – 'A pretty little Castle in the old scotch style'. They enlarged and improved it, decking it out with tartan wallpapers and tartan covers, tartan carpets, even tartan linoleum, and dressed themselves to match in full Highland style.

authority can register their tartans at the office of the Lord Lyon, who is the premier Herald of Scotland, and once this has been done it becomes an offence to sell a tartan which deviates significantly from the sealed pattern. Apart from protecting the sett from careless copying, this means that there is a standard available which makers can work to when scaling up or down. The overall size of a tartan sett depends upon the number of threads in it and their gauge; if, using a given gauge of thread, a larger or smaller sett is required, the weaver has to juggle with the thread count to achieve the desired result, bearing in mind that straight multiplication or division seldom works. The results of reducing a kilt sett to a size suitable for making a necktie and then enlarging that back to kilt size have to be seen to be believed, and to have a standard from which a fresh start can be made every time is most desirable.

Strange as it may seem, it was not until 1963 that any organization existed for the purpose of carrying out research into tartan. In consequence, there was very little sharing of knowledge among the very few people who were interested in tartan, each tending to work in isolation and in the belief that the information at his disposal was all that was to be had; a wise man once said that tartan is a subject the discussion of which generates more heat than light, and under circumstances such as those it is not difficult to see why. However, in 1963, the late Lord Lyon King of Arms, Sir Thomas Innes of Learney, performed the opening ceremony of The Scottish Tartans Information Centre, shortly to be re-named The Scottish Tartans Society, owing, it was said, to the number of people who came in to ask for bus timetables. Housed at first in the Tolbooth at Stirling, it later moved to the Guildhall and thence, when it came under the professional wing of the Dundee Museums Committee, to Broughty Castle, Dundee, the Society made its main work the collecting of material for its own researches, the cataloguing of material in the hands of other bodies and above all, the compilation of a complete index of all the known tartans. A great deal of this has already been accomplished with such success that the Society has become recognized as an authority. Its headquarters is now at Davidson House, Comrie, Perthshire, where it has established its own Museum of Scottish Tartans.

MAKING TARTAN

The Romantics got to work on the subject of making tartan in much the same way as they did on its history, and we can read a lot about the lost secrets of the glens and learn remarkably little from what we read.

Some knowledge of how tartan is made is essential to a proper understanding of it, and the ability to weave is of great help to the serious student, since many of the questions to be answered are concerned with what a fifteenth (or sixteenth, or any other) century Highland weaver would have done in a given case, and the man who has done it is best equipped to solve the problems that arise in this way.

Happily, neither the understanding nor the practice of weaving is a very difficult matter; in the days with which we have to deal 'advanced technology' had not been invented. We need to consider the old, simple, handworked processes rather than to think in terms of modern production methods; these simple processes apply to the amateur hand-weaver today, and so 'is', although it here means 'was', is quite applicable to the descriptions of the weaving processes which follow.

When a fleece comes from the sheep it is dirty and matted and contains quite a lot of foreign matter in the way of twigs and other bits of vegetable material. Therefore, the first process after shearing—or plucking, as is sometimes the case—is to tease out the wool into loose bundles, which frees it from tangles and allows the dirt to fall out. The natural grease of the wool is needed to help the spinning of the thread, so no further cleansing is done at this stage.

A thread *can* be spun from the wool in the teased state, but it is far more usual for the wool to be either carded or combed, according to the type of yarn required. The object of these operations is to produce a bundle of loose fibres from which the thread can be drawn out evenly as it is spun; carding is used for the soft and hairy yarn of the tweed or saxony type and combing gives the smooth hard worsted yarn.

Wool 'cards' are flat, hairbrush-like objects, with hundreds of short wire 'bristles' arranged to face back towards the handle. They are used in pairs, a handful of the teased wool being placed on one and stroked off it with the other. After two or three passes the fibres are evenly fluffed out and can be rolled off the last card in the form of a sausage-shaped bundle called a 'rolag' in which the fibres lie in random directions.

Combs are heavier affairs, built like short floor-brushes but with the handles coming out of the sides instead of at the ends, the 'bristles' in this case being three rows of long iron teeth. One comb is fixed and the other is used to draw the wool through it, straightening the fibres and laying them parallel. Both these activities are considerably aided by warmth, which softens the grease in the wool, and the combs themselves can be warmed, being of sufficient mass to retain the heat.

In terms of social history, the spinning wheel is a fairly recent invention, the use of which spread over the Highlands and Islands between about 1750 and 1850. Prior to this, the spindle, and later the 'muckle wheel', were used for spinning the thread.

The spindle consists of a straight piece of stick, about ten to twelve inches long (25 to 30 cm approximately), with a notch cut in one end and a circular weight, which may be anything from a turned disc of wood or stone to a blob of clay, near the other. To use it, a length of wool is drawn out of the rolag and twisted in the fingers until it is long enough to be tied in a clove hitch round the notched end. Then, with the rolag lying on the back of your left hand and the twisted thread coming out between the thumb and forefinger, you give the spindle a sharp twist with your right hand, so tightening the twist in the thread. As the spindle continues to spin under the influence of the flywheel effect of its weight, you draw out with the right hand, taking care to keep the twist from running up into the rolag; this is done by keeping up the pressure from the thumb and forefinger of the left hand. When the length of spun thread becomes long enough for the spindle to reach the floor, the clove hitch is slipped down to the weight and the thread wound round the spindle, taken over the edge of the weight, once round the projecting part of the spindle and back over the opposite edge of the weight to the top of the spindle where another clove hitch is made and the process begins again. This method of spinning is extremely slow, but with practice a fine and tolerably even thread can be spun, even from wool that has received no more pre-treatment than being teased out and combed with a heavy hair-comb.

Figure 11 : this drawing shows the spinner seated with her spindle, but it can in fact be used just as well on the move, and the women of the Highlands are reputed to have carried on their spinning almost continuously as they went about their other duties.

The operation of the muckle wheel is very similar to that of the spindle. The spindle part of the machine is mounted horizontally in bearings and rotated by means of a large wheel, which is spun by hand, and a driving band. The spinster sets to work in the same way as with the spindle, by twisting a length of thread by hand and clove hitching it to the end; the large wheel is then given a spin and the spinster walks backwards away from it drawing out the thread as she goes. Having spun a short length, she then goes in a quarter circle to the end of the machine and spins the wheel in the opposite direction, which winds the thread on to the spindle. This method of spinning showed a great advance on the spindle and probably spun two or three times as quickly, but it was still very slow indeed and only with the advent of the Saxony type of wheel, in which the twisting and winding went on simultaneously, while the spinster sat at the machine and drove it by a foot treadle, could spinning be said to approach rapidity of production. Even using these wheels, three or four spinsters were required to keep one weaver in operation.

The Saxony type of wheel may take any of several forms, upright or with either horizontal or sloping bed, but all operate in the same way. The yarn feeds into the end of a hollow spinning spindle and out of the side. It is then guided by the horseshoe shaped 'flyer', fixed to the spinning spindle, on to the bobbin, which rotates independently to wind on the thread as it is spun. Both these rotating parts are driven by a double band from the treadle-operated flywheel and a tensioning screw allows the relative speeds of the two to be so varied as to spin and wind at the right rates to give the hardness of twist desired.

When the yarn has been spun, it has to be 'scoured', to remove the grease and enable it to take a dye; a strong soapy lather will attend to this and if desired the spin may be 'set' by stretching the thread on a frame and placing it in boiling water for a few minutes.

It is in the realm of dyeing that we hear most about the lost secrets of the glens and as a result an element of witchcraft has entered into the popular conception of the old-time dyers' art. The secrets were certainly lost, but they cannot have been very secret, because the colours of tartans are nearly universal, without any relation to the districts in which they were made. What really happened was that during the period of the proscription of Highland dress tartan became big business to which the old methods were inappropriate; no doubt, the old dyers had their own methods, which they used regularly and did not write down for this reason, so that when they died their recipes died with them. However, this does not mean that they cannot be recovered, nor that 'eye of newt' and other choice additives were necessary in order to achieve the desired shade of colour.

Natural dyes can produce beautiful colours, brilliant yet soft, but there was and is nothing magic about them. Modern synthetic dyes can match them accurately (and have done so for some of the illustrations in this book) and they are much more permanent.

An infusion of almost any plant will yield a dye, usually yellow, sometimes without further assistance although in most cases the addition of a simple and easily prepared chemical, termed a 'mordant', is required. Bracken, for instance, can be used to produce a yellow dye, heather a yellowish green, walnut bark a black, lichens a scarlet-red, sloes a blue; and one can get up to nine different colours from blaeberries. Typical mordants are alum, copper sulphate and copperas (ferrous sulphate), each of which has a modifying effect on the colour given by a particular plant; cream of tartar, which in its crude form, argol, occurs naturally on the insides of wine-vats and wine-bottles, is sometimes used as a brightening agent. Present-day practice in vegetable dyeing is to mordant the wool first, keeping it damp and in the dark for a day or two before the actual dyeing is done, but it is probable that our Highland dyers did the whole job at one go, stewing mordant, dye-plant and wool together until the desired shade was reached. We know that in some cases this took several days of slow cooking over a peat fire—and can envy people who were able to build such a fire where they wanted and leave it to get on with its work! I have to fit in my own dyeing experiments around the cookery and risk being chased out of the kitchen and away from the gas stove at some critical moment. There is a great deal of room for serious experiment with native dyestuffs and the proper recording of results, and anyone who wishes to embark on it, may like to know that a large vacuum jar, which will keep the solutions hot enough to be active for at least twenty-four hours, is a very good substitute for a peat fire.

When the wool is dyed and dried it is ready to be woven—so long as it has not gone back to a dirty grey, as has been known to happen. However, before we begin to weave there are several preliminary jobs to be undertaken, not the least important of which is to see how weaving works.

A loom need be no more than a stout frame, or even a piece of board, upon which the lengthways threads, called the 'warp', are stretched, so that the 'weft' threads can be darned across between them. This is all right for pieces of cloth about six inches (about 15 cm) square, woven

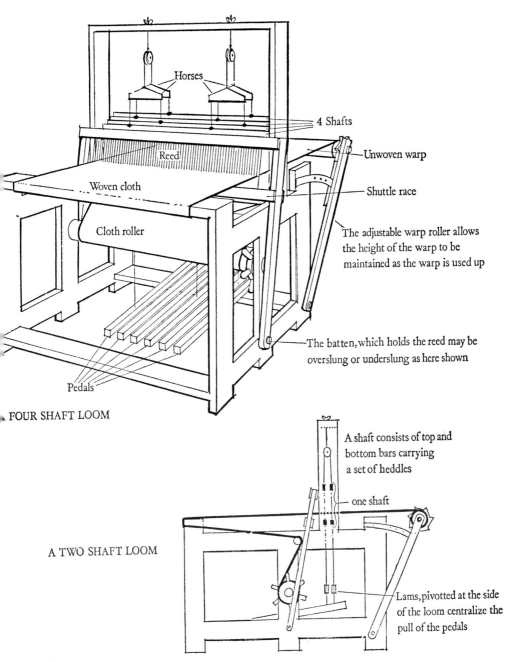

Horses

4 Shafts

Reed

Unwoven warp

Shuttle race

Woven cloth

Cloth roller

The adjustable warp roller allows
the height of the warp to be
maintained as the warp is used up

The batten, which holds the reed may be
overslung or underslung as here shown

Pedals

FOUR SHAFT LOOM

A shaft consists of top and
bottom bars carrying
a set of heddles

one shaft

A TWO SHAFT LOOM

Lams, pivotted at the side
of the loom centralize the
pull of the pedals

Figure 12

in rug wool, but it becomes tedious and eventually impossible as the yarn becomes finer and the piece of cloth bigger; in addition, there is absolutely no production potential about this way of doing it.

What we may perhaps be permitted to call a 'proper' loom suitable for weaving cloth in reasonable quantity, will be rather different from this. Whether it be a small 'table' loom, suitable for making scarves, or a full-size 'hand' loom, it will be equipped with rollers fore and aft, so that a moderately long warp may be put on and the cloth wound on as it is woven, and there will be some mechanical means—levers for the table loom and pedals for the hand loom—of raising and lowering the warp threads in pre-arranged groups so that a shuttle carrying the weft thread can be passed through the gap so-formed, which is called the 'shed'. A further necessary part in the practical loom is the 'reed', an assembly of evenly spaced metal strips that serves the dual purpose of spacing the warp threads and beating in the weft. Given a loom fully set up and ready to start work, all we need do to weave is to press the pedals or levers alternately, and pass the shuttle back and forth and beat at each pass.

The '2/2' or 'plain' twill in which tartan is usually woven calls for what is known as a 'four shaft' loom. The 'shaft' consists of an upper and lower bar between which run the heddles (a series of vertical cords or wires, each with a loop, or 'eye', in the middle through which a warp thread is passed) which raise and lower the warp threads to form the shed; it is the raising of the threads in staggered pairs that produces the distinctive diagonal ribbing of tartan, so clearly seen where contrasting colours cross.

It has long been the custom to make the pattern of a tartan in two halves reversing about their end stripes so that each section of the pattern is the mirror image of the adjoining sections. Further, the pattern is made the same in both directions of the cloth, so that if properly woven at the same number of threads per inch (per 25 mm) for both warp and weft the pattern will be truly square and the diagonal ribbing of the twill weave will run from corner to corner of each square of colour.

A side effect of this is that each coloured stripe or line in the weft will cross its counterpart in the warp, so that each colour of the tartan,

Plate 14: often a single design feature or motif can be seen to run through a whole series of related tartans. The MacDonald tartans, in which the motif consists of a broad bar flanked by a narrow one on each side, provide a very clear example of this. In the dark CLAN MACDONALD tartan (right) the motif is subtly concealed between the lines of the red overchecks on the green and blue grounds, but in the other setts shown it is more obvious. They are LORD OF THE ISLES (top left) which becomes MacDonald of Sleat if the black overcheck is omitted; LORD OF THE ISLES HUNTING (centre left), made in two shades of green although the first publication showed it in blue and green; and MACDONALD OF KINGSBURGH (bottom left), taken from a relic of the '45 (here shown in modern colours).

Plates 15 and 16: Two Scottish Castles

The two castles illustrated here exemplify the contrast between the early Highland strongholds dating from the days when a stone dwelling of two or more storeys was virtually a 'castle', and the later style – elegant, and sometimes even fanciful, in appearance – with its hanging turrets and conical roofs. Above is Carnassary Castle in Argyllshire, stoutly built though now in ruins; to the left, Glamis Castle, like a drawing from a book of fairytales.

Plate 17: in the BLACK WATCH tartan (top left) the motif is the broad band and pair of lines that bound every second blue square. It has long been popular with designers and appears with great frequency in red as well as dark tartans. Its inclusion in the dark HUNTING STEWART tartan (top right) is probably an error of long standing; in its original form this tartan belongs to the Mackintosh group.

MACLACHLAN (bottom left) and MACNAB (bottom right) are, as can be seen, Black Watch with the colours changed, the latter, for example, being patterned in dark green, scarlet and crimson, where Black Watch is patterned in blue, green and black.

as well as appearing solid where it crosses itself, will be mixed in equal quantities with every other colour; solid colours cannot appear side by side, but always join corner to corner. It is this blending of colours that accounts for the multi-coloured effect of tartan, for the number of mixtures increases rapidly as single colours are added. A check pattern of two colours gives two pure colours and one mixture, four colours gives four pure and six mixtures, and seven colours, the largest number usually encountered, gives seven plus twenty-one, a total of twenty-eight colours.

Although the conventions of tartan design are usually observed, it is not *necessary* either for the pattern to reverse or for it to be the same in both warp and weft. Some eighteenth-century Hebridean tartans are both non-reversing and different in warp and weft, and a few early nineteenth-century commercial tartans, while otherwise following the rules, used different colours in warp and weft. Generally, though, the worst that can happen is for a tartan to be non-reversing. Plate 5 facing page 57 illustrates the regular reversing pattern, the non-reversing pattern, and a compound type with features of both.

The name by which this type of pattern was known to the early tartan trade was **Cheek**, and this was generally mistranscribed by ardent but unknowledgeable collectors as 'Check' with the consequence that some tartans were completely misrendered as reversing setts when they should have been non-reversing. Happily, most of these were simple check patterns anyway, and had no clan significance, but the occurrence of this kind of error, perpetrated by people who should have known better, shows how careful one must be, and how important it is to make every possible check on one's findings before accepting any statement about tartans. In short, suspect everybody of incompetence, but most of all, suspect yourself.

TARTAN DESIGN

As tartan is a cloth of regular pattern, woven in self-coloured yarn (that is, dyed before weaving, not afterward) and of twill weave, we can say with some assurance, albeit only for the purpose of drawing a family tree, that the small black-and-white check pattern which we call Shepherd's Plaid is the ancestor of all tartan patterns.

However, while it is probably the simplest way of ornamenting a woven fabric, it does not allow of much variety in the pattern and if the size of the checks is much enlarged it very soon becomes unacceptably loud while remaining a trifle undistinguished in appearance.

Whether the first makers of shepherd's plaid were able to dye their yarn we cannot tell—to a largely pastoral people with adequate supplies of naturally coloured wool from their 'white' and 'black' sheep close to hand, it may simply have been not worth the trouble—but it is certain that the first step towards a recognizable tartan design did not come until colour was incorporated. Colour gave a softer contrast to the check pattern and the checks could be made much larger without offending the eye. The red and black MacGregor tartan now called Rob Roy is known to have been popular for trews about two hundred and fifty years ago and there is no reason to suppose that its origin was not considerably earlier. This pattern could be safely made in squares up to about three inches across (about 7·5 cm) and had at one time a companion named MacLauchlan in red and green. There may perhaps have been a touch of humour in the naming of Wilsons' No. 224 black and green check, Robin Hood. Wilsons exploited the two-colour check to the maximum extent that a limited range of colour would permit but there is not a great deal of scope for this type of pattern and the line of development soon ran out.

There are three simple ways of enlivening a check pattern. One is to add an overcheck line to one or both of the main checks, another is to add a third colour, and the third is to multiply the number of checks of one colour, placing them close together on the other, which then becomes a ground with stripes.

Overchecks add considerably to the scope available to the designer of

90

tartan, since they may be single or multiple lines and in the latter case may be either all the same colour or of different colours; they can even alternate from one square to another, so long as the alternation is regular. Strangely, this way of doing things does not seem to have appealed to the old weavers, and it was in the nineteenth century that most tartans of this type came to the fore. Overchecks, however, are a constantly recurring device, and their application is not by any means confined to the gingering up of check patterns. There are many examples: Plate 14, facing page 88, for instance, as described below.

The second variation gives us the basis of what is probably by far the greater number of our dark tartans, the blue/black/green check, which usually has the blue and green squares about twice as wide as the black bars which separate them. Overchecks are much used here also, and are seen in the four red lines in each coloured square that denote the MacDonald tartan (Plate 14, facing page 88) and outline the design motif (of which more later), and the compound arrangement of Black Watch (Plate 17, facing page 89), which has pairs of black lines around the edge of one blue square and across the middle of the next.

Black Watch fathers a number of direct derivatives, mostly made by the addition of overchecks, and also passes on a motif for use by designers outside its own context. By far the most interesting of the direct derivatives of Black Watch are two which demonstrate very well the way in which a tartan can be changed out of recognition by simple alterations of colour. In MacLachlan, the green of Black Watch is changed to blue and the blue to red; the black overcheck on the green becomes green on blue, but this is a minor matter. In MacNab blue becomes scarlet, black becomes crimson and blue becomes green; the effect is to turn what is the darkest of tartans into one of the most savagely brilliant. Both are shown with Black Watch in Plate 17 facing page 89.

Among the direct derivatives of Black Watch are all the British military tartans except that of the Cameron Highlanders, Cameron of Erracht, which is MacDonald-based. Apart from the Gordons, who took yellow overchecks to the green instead of black, and the Seaforths, whose Mackenzie tartan with its white and red overchecks was also taken by the Highland Light Infantry, there were numerous

Fencible regiments who varied the parent 42nd pattern in similar ways.

Stryppes upone ane Fylde were greatly beloved by the Sobieski brothers, who based about half of the designs shown in *Vestiarium Scoticum* on such simple schemes, some with three stripes, some with four, some with all stripes the same colour, some with the colours paired off. The point that these tartans cannot be accepted as ancient, or even as older than about the first third of the nineteenth century, has already been laboured sufficiently, but it is perhaps worth pointing out that some of them can be taken as mangled versions of proper tartans that were around at the time the various Sobieski MSS were 'discovered'. Uninteresting as the Sobieski striped patterns generally are, this *need* not be so. The much older MacKay and Ross tartans are both fundamentally of this class (Plate 20, facing page 97); tartan design is a very serious art form, and the difference between a good design and a bad one can be very striking indeed.

Also to be counted among the striped patterns is one whose authenticity is vouched for probably more strongly than any other, which we now call Mackintosh (Plate 5, facing page 57), though Wilsons first named it Caledonian Sett, which perhaps only goes to show its widespread use: they tried 'Lovat, or Fraser Tartan' on it as well. The Mackintosh tartan has interest other than its age though, for the 1819 Key Pattern Book of William Wilson and Son contains enough named patterns based upon it to show clearly that it was the weavers who made the clan tartans and that they did it by copying from the man next door and adding their own variations to his pattern; from Inverness and the Mackintosh country, through the Great Glen to Fort William and the edge of Lochaber, this red tartan with two wide green stripes and two narrower purple ones formed the basis of tartans ascribed (in 1819) to clans whose mutual hostility was such that in 1850 they would not have considered wearing even remotely similar tartans; clearly, if these tartans had been in long-standing use (either because the local weavers were too lazy to change, or because the people liked them) the feeling for clan tartans was less strong than it became later.

The question of the 'lifting' of designs, or parts of them, brings us back to the subject of motifs, briefly touched upon already. One of the least obvious, and consequently one of the most interesting, examples of a motif in a tartan design is that which is *outlined* by the red lines on the dark ground of the MacDonald tartans, Clan, Glengarry and Clanranald; while this pattern of a broad line with a narrow one close by on each side is in the ground colour of the 'parent' design, it appears in a small scale, in white on the Lord of the Isles Hunting tartan and in yellow in MacDonald of Kingsburgh, and to a large scale in green on the red ground of MacDonald of the Isles and MacDonald of Sleat and others. The motif can be seen in the MacDonald tartans illustrated in Plate 14 facing page 88. To what extent the motif can be taken to be a MacDonald one, or whether it is merely the device of a MacDonald weaver is, of course, unknown, but it appears in a number of old tartans of MacDonald attribution and in few others, although the Sobieski brothers incorporated it in their MacArthur tartan.

The motif of the Black Watch tartan, a broad bar with two lines close to one side of it (Plate 17, facing page 89), is a rather different case and is frequently used as a design device in its own right, appearing in many tartans quite unrelated to the tartan from which it is taken. This was another design feature much favoured by the Sobieskis and accounts for another ten of the designs first found in *Vestiarium Scoticum*. But it was a well-established idea even at the time of the embodiment of the 43rd Regiment of Foot—the first title of the Black Watch, when it was formed in 1739 from the six Independent Companies of the Highland Watch—and appears in at least one relic that survived long enough to be copied and so preserved. This was the tartan now called Hunting MacRae, taken from a piece of a kilt believed to have been worn at Sheriffmuir in 1715.

Although the red Mackintosh tartan (Plate 5) is so widely used as the basis for others, it does not stop at that, for this tartan also has a motif—two broad bars with a narrower one each side of the pair—which finds its way into a few other patterns. Noteworthy among these is the tartan designed about 1907 for use in the plaids of pipers of the 1st Battalion, 1st Gurkha Rifles, erroneously known as Childers Universal Tartan and equally erroneously recommended for wear by the English and other non-Scots who wish to take a tartan (Plate 5, facing page 57). This design is arrived at by changing the colours of the Mackintosh tartan, red to black, blue to ash green and green to beech green; the central blue line becomes red. Hunting Stewart in its earliest form had only a single black line at the blue end of the pattern, instead of the full Black Watch motif now incorporated (Plate 17, facing page 89), and then showed an interesting use of the Mackintosh motif, which appeared in the four black bars at one end of the pattern and in blue at the other. Where the second black line came from, to complete the Black Watching of this tartan, nobody knows; the Sobieskis were playing with it at one time, and may have added this feature to bring it into line with the other Stewart tartans, both real and of their own invention, but these particular dogs have a bad enough name for almost any tartan evil-doing to be attributed to them, which is probably unfair.

Another family of tartans deriving, like the Mackintosh group, from a common ancestor, is that of which the best-known example is Royal Stewart (Plate 21, facing page 104). These mostly share the feature of a red ground with a light blue edge and include MacDuff, MacNaughton (Plate 21), Sinclair, an obsolete Menzies tartan (Plate 21), Prince Charles Edward Stuart, MacPherson, and Caledonia (Plate 21); Macbeth is distinguished by a blue ground with yellow edges, being otherwise the same as Royal Stewart, and a black-grounded version of the Royal Stewart tartan has become popular. The origin of the Royal Stewart tartan is unknown. In his book *Children of the Mist*, published in 1890, Lord Archibald Campbell wrote:

'We have the Duke of St Albans' coat, now at Bestwood, which was worn by Charles II at his wedding, the ribbons of which are of Royal Stuart tartan.'

A footnote reads:

'See *Records of Argyll*, page 446. Duchess of St Albans' letter to Mrs, now Lady Millais.'

Sir John Millais was knighted in 1885, so the Duchess's letter must have been written before that date.

No one, however, seems to have checked the ribbons or been able to verify this story. There is no record of the Royal Stewart sett having borne that name before the nineteenth century—little that it even existed. As Donald Stewart points out, General Stewart of Garth, who stage-managed George IV's Scottish visit in 1822 and costumed him in

94

'Royal Stewart', wrote in 1815 that he had no knowledge of *any* Stewart tartan; it may perhaps have acquired the name from George IV's wearing it on the celebrated visit. One may note that the Duchess was writing at a time when tartans were all the rage and the Clan Tartan idea firmly entrenched in Victorian belief.

There are several pieces of this tartan, and the nearly related Prince Charles Edward pattern, in existence which were, it is claimed, worn by the Prince and his adherents during the 1745 campaigns; and if these claims are true—we cannot say that they are not, nor that they are —Prince Charles Edward would seem to be the earliest form in which the tartan appeared; this would also account for its becoming the Royal tartan.

Although a great deal of borrowing of patterns and motifs clearly went on in the days when each village had its own weaver, catering for the needs of the villagers, it must not be thought that tartan design was limited to plagiarism; there are beautiful and original specimens to be seen in many museums, public and private. Even at the beginning of the commercial exploitation of tartan, Wilsons were making a number of patterns whose only common feature was their considerable complication. Patterns such as Aberdeen and Dundee, now achieving popularity under the wholly spurious designation of 'district' tartans, were woven at a pitch of about 65 threads to the inch (25 mm approximately), and Aberdeen had over a hundred and twenty separate stripes to a width of nineteen inches (about 50 cm). These patterns were termed 'Old Superfine Tartan Setts' in 1819, and later patterns were neither so finely woven nor so distinguished in appearance, but there were few that were ugly in the same way that many modern designs are.

To make one of these old designs, from yarn which, although nowhere near as fine as Wilsons' coarsest, is dyed to match their colours, is a never-failing thrill and shows the weaver perhaps more clearly than anything that our Highland ancestors cannot all have been blood-thirsty ruffians; at least, not all of the time.

Many tartans, notably those derived from Black Watch by the addition of overchecks, but also including Hunting Stewart (Plate 17), are completely symmetrical except for the overchecks being in alternating colours; reference to a specimen or a photograph of one of these will show that such a simple change renders the tartan non-reversing within the meaning of the Act, but this is a very minor infringement of the rules which are quite seriously violated by two well-known tartans, Buchanan (Plate 3, facing page 56) and Ancient MacMillan. Both these derive from the tartan recorded by James Logan under the name of Buchanan and stated by him to have been worn by both clans alike. As included in the appendix to *The Scottish Gael*, this was a small pattern remarkable for the comparatively large amounts of yellow and light blue used. Later, Logan collaborated with Robert McIan, the artist, in producing *The Clans of the Scottish Highlands*, a series of coloured plates of figures in Highland costume with historical commentaries, which was published over the period 1843 to 1849. It was from McIan's two different, but both inaccurate, drawings of tartan for the plates entitled respectively *Buchanan* and *MacMillan* that these two tartans come. It was not until 1950, when Donald C. Stewart (*The Setts of the Scottish Tartans*) pointed out this aberration in respect of the Buchanan tartan that it began to be made again to the original pattern, although this had been available to manufacturers since 1831.

An eye for colour and for the proper blending thereof is an important attribute of the designer of tartans, and both the limited range and the softness of the colours that were obtained from the old natural dyes were of great help in that respect, however much the dyers may have wished for more and stronger colours at the time. Synthetic dyestuffs, which began to appear in the middle of the nineteenth century, soon repaired these 'deficiencies'; scarlet became so vivid that it has been described as lighting up at night, the deeper shade of red called rose turned to crimson, blue went nearly black and green came close behind. Tartan was on the way to becoming fancy dress, and so far from being the right dress for the hill because of its camouflaging quality, became impossible to wear if any kind of concealment was necessary; thus, hunting tartans were born. The basic principle behind

Plate 18: a hand loom with fly-shuttle and eight shafts, from the Angus Folk Collection in Glamis

Plate 19: a cottage in Sutherland, ruined now, but built in the traditional Highland style, small and attractively simple

Plate 20: all tartans are made up of crossing lines and stripes, but Vestiarium Scoticum inclined to specialize in rather uninteresting layouts. MACLEOD OF LEWIS (upper left) is typical of about three dozen of the designs in that work which differed in little but colour. MACKAY (lower left) is an earlier design of this kind which shows that a tartan need not be either complicated or multi-coloured to look attractive. ROSS (upper right) adds a small amount of complication to the basic theme; this design was at one time made in plain purple on a green ground. BLANKET SETT, made by Wilsons of Bannockburn and shown here with its border, is a typical arisaid sett. (It was from such setts as these, originally worn by women, that the modern dress tartans developed; their use for men's evening wear is anomalous.) This pattern was made only 19 inches wide with a border on one side, so that two pieces could be joined to make the width of a plaid.

the design of these is quite simple and consists merely of replacing a bright red background with green, blue or brown; some other small alterations may be necessary, for example to cope with a green stripe formerly on the red ground, but these do not hide the resemblance of such a hunting tartan to its clan parent. It is interesting to take a piece of a red clan tartan and its hunting version in 'modern' colours, and compare them with a piece of the red tartan in 'ancient' colours; generally it will be seen that the latter appears much more suitable for use on the hill.

Not all hunting tartans are plays on the clan tartan, however; several clans have dark tartans as well as bright ones to choose from, and these need not bear any close resemblance to each other.

Another manifestation of mid-nineteenth century enthusiasm is the 'dress' tartan; like the hunting tartan, this is contrived from the clan pattern, but this time the ground is white. One possible explanation of this is, as I have already mentioned, that it came from a confusion of words. The old dress of the Highland women, the arisaid, was invariably of white or light-coloured material with a few widely spaced lines of colour. The idea of a white tartan used for women's dresses was taken and wedded to the clan tartan to make a new design for men's evening dress, with such anomalous results as Dress Black Watch. The women's tartans never had any pretentions to be clan patterns, and if considered for men's wearing these modern dress tartans can only be seen as a mistake of some over-enthusiastic imagination; for women, however, they are entirely appropriate and represent a logical extension of the old idea joined to the new.

Those clans which can boast bright *and* dark tartans usually refer to the bright one as the dress tartan, and these should not be confused with the white dress tartans.

Several tartans exist in a form in which the pattern has been reduced to plain black and white, and it is commonly held that these are special funeral wear or mourning tartans; if this is so, it is unlikely that they are of any age: the Highland clansman was too close to death in his daily business to worry about a special tartan to commemorate it, even if he could afford a wardrobe that extended to more than one kilt.

WHAT TARTAN SHOULD I WEAR?

After the question 'What does a Scotsman wear under his kilt?' the demand 'What tartan should *I* wear?' is probably the one most frequently asked by interested visitors to Scotland. Much ingenuity has gone into the formulation of 'rights' to tartans—a desperate tartan hunter can be just as desperate as a tartan merchant who sees the prospect of a customer escaping—but with all this there remain some people whose names are not on the *What Is My Tartan?* lists, or who are not convinced by the arguments that seek to assign them a tartan.

There is nothing to prevent anyone who seriously wants a tartan of his own from having one designed, or if he wants an easier way out, from choosing a pattern from among the many available that have never been adopted as clan tartans. The difficulty in both these cases is to get the cloth made, for there are very few firms who will weave even as short a piece as a kilt length of a special tartan; the alternative is to take up one of the established 'general use' tartans, such as Hunting Stewart, Caledonia or Jacobite. The first of these (Plate 17, facing page 89) appears always to have been a tartan for general use, in spite of its name, the second (Plate 21, facing page 104) was originally No. 155 in Wilsons' Key Pattern Book and so is of respectable antiquity, and the political implications of the last now carry little weight, so any can be regarded as satisfactory for the purpose.

Black Watch (Plate 17, facing page 89) and the 1st Gurkha Rifles tartan, under its misnomer of Childers Universal (Plate 5, facing page 57), have both been recommended, in various places, for indiscriminate civilian wear; it is my purely personal opinion that a military tartan should only be worn by people who have a tangible right to do so as members of the unit concerned or of other units which wear its tartan or, among civilians, members of clans which have early associations with the unit, as, in the case of Black Watch, the Munros, Grants and Campbells.

Another tartan that comes in for occasional misuse in this respect is Royal Stewart (Plate 21, facing page 104). It is probable that the 'Royal' title is nothing more than a name bestowed by the tartan trade, for the

Stewart monarchs were of Lowland extraction and their troubles with their Highland subjects seem unlikely to have led them to go out of their way to pay the Highlanders the compliment of assuming Highland dress to the extent of having a special Royal tartan. Nevertheless, the tartan bore the name in 1819 and was worn by George IV on the occasion of his visit to Edinburgh in 1822, so it clearly had then some claim to exclusiveness. More recently, George V made it known that he considered that, he being the Chief of the British nation, his clansmen were entitled to wear his tartan; however, his son, George VI, reversed this decision, and the tartan became exclusively Royal once again, for use by the Royal House only; so far as is known, no further pronouncement has been made. The present Royal family seem generally to favour the darker tartans, Old Stewart and Hunting Stewart, but are sometimes seen in the Balmoral tartan, which is emphatically their own. This tartan was designed by the Prince Consort for Queen Victoria and is exclusive to the Royal family; it should not be possible for any 'outsider' to purchase it and, although mistakes can happen, it is unlikely to be seen in the gift shops. There *is* a story that an outfitter who received an order from Balmoral for eleven ties in the tartan, himself ordered a dozen from the manufacturer and later found the last one hanging up in the 'casual sale' rack outside his shop, but this is likely to be apocryphal.

People who neither have a tartan nor any pretensions to one, and those who bear straightforward clan names, are the easiest to serve. Recognizable alternative spellings of clan names cause little trouble; but difficulties begin to creep in with sept names (septs are small groups within major clans), become worse as we move on to names that are only associated with a clan, and get worse still as the relationship becomes more remote.

The Lord Lyon King of Arms, who is the Chief Herald of Scotland, has laid it down that the *right* to wear any tartan is vested only in the bearers of the name that goes with it; this is all very well so far as it goes, but it is of little help to those whose claim to a tartan is based on the fact that Grannie wore it, or something like that.

Turning to sept names, these are generally peculiar to one or two clans, and it has become the custom for members of the sept to wear the clan tartan if the sept has none of its own; in those cases where the same sept name belongs to two or more clans, it is desirable to know to which clan one is affiliated, but there is usually some family tradition which can answer that question even if it cannot give great detail of descent. It may be noted here that specialist tradesmen could also form septs within their clan.

General names with clan connections fall into much the same class as sept names when it comes to finding tartans to go with them, with the difference that there are many more of them and the connections are often much more remote.

In the troubled past, a particularly troublesome clan might be deprived of its name, by law, as a means of breaking down its unity of feeling and mutual support among its members; this led to the clansmen taking new surnames, so building up a body of related names (and a reservoir of tartan sales). The Lamonts and the MacGregors are particularly well-endowed this way, the former having sixty names related to it and the latter ninety, including such as Black, Brown and White; bearers of names related in this way, if they really want to be sure of their ground, should indulge in at least the minimum of ancestor research.

Lastly we come to the great majority, the ones who can only claim Grannie's tartan; for these, honesty is the only remedy! The early records of the tartan industry make it very clear that when first tartan went on sale in the shops, people chose whatever they fancied in the way of a pattern, and modern study has shown equally clearly that whatever may have been the general practice, the *idea* of a rigidly defined system of uniform tartans is comparatively new. There can surely then be no objection to wearing Grannie's tartan for reasons of sentiment and respect, so long as no corns are trodden on and the tartan is not claimed as of right. There is some support for this view to be found in the portrait of Norman, 22nd of MacLeod, to be seen at Dunvegan Castle, in which the Chief is wearing a plaid that has been identified as Murray of Tullibardine, one explanation of the apparent anomaly being that Norman's grandmother was of that family.

Probably because of Martin's remarks about being able to guess the place of a man's residence from a sight of his plaid, but certainly nurtured by Wilsons who, apart from having one or two patterns that just might have had some local affinities, named a range of their own designs after towns and cities, there has grown up a range of what are called 'district' tartans, which are supposed to be those worn by people who did not belong to a clan and merely resided in a particular district. Perhaps not a very likely theory, it does give the tartan hunter a last chance and many of the revivals, if made in the original colours, are quite beautiful designs.

As time goes on, the range of 'district' tartans will probably increase, for tartan is a live business and the pattern has an undeniable attraction; what we must hope is that designers of new tartans will make a good job of it; old-style tartans, with their firm, bold designs and colours that were meant to be seen, were of a beauty that completely escapes the modern, rather spindly designs in colours often chosen for their pseudo-symbolism rather than for their appearance.

A TARTAN TREE

Much amusement can be gained, and the tartan-spotting eye given good training, by spending an occasional hour or two in playing with colour strips and looking for relationships between the tartans. In this game, care must be taken to avoid attaching too much significance to relationships when found; tartans based on Mackintosh may have been worn by clans inhabiting lands on both sides of the Great Glen from one end to the other, but this does not mean that all the clans were related, or even allied. What it probably does mean is that some weaver in the north-east made the simple basic pattern and when others saw it they added their own twiddly bits and offered the result to their own customers.

It was not only the weavers of the glens and the clachans who indulged in this. Wilsons were not the original inventors of tartan even though their name crops up so often as to suggest that they may have had a hand in it, so it is reasonable to suppose that some of the tartans were around before their time; in fact, they showed themselves to be fully alive to the needs and potentialities of their business, and there would be nothing to be surprised about if we were to find that they had made a point of seeking old fragments and bringing them back to life.

SOME INTERESTING TARTANS

'He was then barefooted,' wrote John Cameron, describing Bonnie Prince Charlie as a fugitive in Highland dress, 'had an old black kilt coat on, a plaid, a philabeg and waistcoat, a dirty shirt and a long red beard.'

In most minds, tartans and Jacobite romance are fairly thoroughly mixed, and it often seems that the number of plaids worn by Bonnie Prince Charlie must at least rival the number of beds in which Queen Elizabeth slept.

However, among the surviving relics of the last great Jacobite bid to regain the throne of Great Britain there are a few of which we can say just a little more than that they are 'supposed' to have been worn by the Prince, although very little of their history may be known. In this category we may include the coat worn by a member of the Prince's personal suite at Culloden, and a plaid found on the battlefield after the rout of the Jacobite army. The pattern of the plaid was reproduced by D. W. Stewart in the illustrations for *Old and Rare Scottish Tartans*.

Two relics directly associated with the Prince are a plaid given by him to the Countess of Eglinton, as a memento of his stay at Holyrood Palace, and the MacDonald of Kingsburgh tartan (Plate 14, facing page 88), reconstructed by D. W. Stewart from the surviving fragment of a waistcoat given to the Prince by Kingsburgh during his travels in the Highlands after Culloden.

As the Prince considered the MacDonald of Kingsburgh pattern rather too striking for a fugitive, he exchanged it with one Malcolm MacLeod who, before he was himself captured, managed to hide the garment in a cleft in a rock; upon his release, a year later, he was able to recover the remnants, and these ultimately found their way to the Advocates' Library, in Edinburgh.

Turning now to a more modern tartan, MacKerrell underlines another lesson.

The MacKerrell pattern has been around for some time. The thread count was originally given in one-eighth inch units (3 mm approximately) and written in two columns, as shown overleaf:

Thread Count

W $\frac{3}{4}$	W $\frac{3}{4}$
A 5	A 5
P 9	P 9
Y $\frac{1}{2}$	R $\frac{1}{2}$
P 9	P 9
A 5	A 5

(W means white, A azure, P purple, Y yellow and R red-scarlet)

If this count is read as one column for warp and one for weft, we get red lines one way and yellow the other; if it is read across, from left to right, we get alternating red and yellow lines in the purple. (Sample thread counts are given and explained in Appendix 1, pages 111–16, and should prove helpful.)

Both interpretations have been tried, which makes for confusion; to my mind the latter is more likely. The thread count for the half sett would thus be:

W	A	P	R/Y
6	40	72	4

with the white and the red/yellow being the pivot stripes on which the pattern reverses. (The whole width of the pivot stripes is given.) An additional source of possible confusion is that the scribbled figures 5 and 9 in the original thread count could have been mis-read for one another, which gives us two more versions, one with equal and the other with unequal checks. Tartanology is full of such pitfalls.

MacDonald of Glenaladale, the Glenfinnan tartan, is a reimport from Canada, whither the original was taken in 1792. One of several pieces of similar design, this was copied in Canada and the copy came into the hands of Lieutenant-Colonel Iain Cameron Taylor, Historical Secretary of the National Trust for Scotland, who set about putting it back into production as being the tartan appropriate to the locality of the Trust's centre at Glenfinnan.

Finally, we come to three tartans which show clearly how existing tartans could be modified to answer the call for more new designs at the time of the Revival. These are illustrated in Plate 24, facing page 105.

Plate 21: motifs are generally independent of colour, but this group of tartans, all designed around a red square with a blue border, provides the exception. Simplest is a now obsolete MENZIES tartan (lower right) which, by very little manipulation, can become MACNAUGHTON (lower left). The origin of ROYAL STEWART (upper right) is unknown, but it seems improbable that the royal Stewarts knew about it. CALEDONIA (upper left) began life as Wilson's No. 155, a variant on No. 43 (see Plates 8 and 12); the name appears to be a modern attachment.

Plate 22 (above): 'Highland Chieftain', a portrait dating from about 1680; this is the earliest known painting which shows a Scot wearing a broadsword

Plate 23 (right): the stone at Culloden, commemorating the defeat of the Highlanders and the ending of a way of life for ever.

THE BATTLE
OF CULLODEN
WAS FOUGHT ON THIS MOOR
16TH APRIL 1746.

THE GRAVES OF THE
GALLANT HIGHLANDERS
WHO FOUGHT FOR
SCOTLAND & PRINCE CHARLIE
ARE MARKED BY THE NAMES
OF THEIR CLANS.

Plate 24a: the black and white CLAN TARTAN is reckoned to be the oldest of the MACPHERSON setts, believed to have been taken from a shawl given by Simon, Lord Lovat, to his daughter when she married Ewen MacPherson of Cluny.

Plate 24b: it is not surprising that Wilsons' No. 6, or CLARK, tartan (about 1847) should follow the same scheme of light and dark squares separated by groups of three lines, for the Clarks are an acknowledged MacPherson sept.

Plate 24c: Wilsons' GIPSY tartan also follows the same scheme as the MacPherson. The connection is obscure — but the famous freebooter James MacPherson was the son of a gipsy woman, and the Wilsons were astute business men.

The black and grey MacPherson tartan is also made in black and white, and in this form is claimed to be the oldest of all the MacPherson tartans; the Clarks are an acknowledged sept of the MacPhersons, so we may take it that their tartan, put out by Wilsons between 1820 and 1847, did not occur by accident. Gipsy cannot be accounted for in this way, and we have to assume that it was merely a matter of changing the colours of an existing design to meet the need for new patterns. In the early post-proscription boom, when demand was enormous and the Clan Tartan system had not reached its later standards of rigidity, new patterns were commonly produced in this way or by similar small alterations to existing designs.

A SPREAD OF TARTAN

Wherever the Highlander has gone, he has taken his tartans with him, and wherever he has settled there has been a tendency for new designs to develop.

Units affiliated to the British Army, like the Gurkha regiments, have formed pipe bands and adopted tartan, and we have already met with the misnamed Childers Universal Tartan, designed for one of these. (It is shown in the colour plate, facing page 57.) In the nineteen-thirties, two designs were produced for the Jahore Regiment; although they look a bit over-bright for our Highland taste, these would look well under the brighter light of Indian skies.

America has also produced its crop and one of these is Polaris, a Black Watch variant, designed in 1964 for the crew of the U.S. submarine of that name; another example is the tartan of the New York Fire Brigade Pipe Band, produced at about the same time. This simple design is very closely related to our own Hunting Rose, although I do not know whether this be accident or planned; often a new tartan will carry the name of its designer into an entirely different field, or the basis will be chosen to perpetuate the name of some individual.

Canada has been by far the most prolific of any country in the production of new tartans in recent years and now has many provincial and district tartans, as well as a fair crop of celebratory designs and some for Societies and general wear.

To represent the British Isles in the race, there are the Manx, Cornish and Welsh tartans, and Ireland has fairly recently begun to produce designs based on traditional patterns. The Scot may say of these that they are merely attempts to climb upon the tartan band-waggon by those who have no justification for so doing, and to some extent he will be right, for it was in the Highlands that tartan reached its peak of development, and in Scotland where it achieved its greatest significance; whether that significance is based on truth or falsehood matters not, for it now exists. But the continued production of new tartans shows that tartan is still alive, and as long as it remains alive it will be worn, by some in accordance with clan usage, by others by mistake or just because they like it. Let us not be too hard on those who appear to transgress our own opinions in these matters and instead, greet the stranger wearing 'our' tartan, not as a usurper but as a potential ally.

The design and making of tartan cannot stand still. The clans died at Culloden, but in spite of the Government's rigid ban on the wearing of Highland dress, the tradition of tartan survived, and today it is a live and growing matter; let us be glad of that.

APPENDICES

THE STUDIOUS APPROACH
TO TARTAN

It cannot be expected that every reader of this book will immediately feel the impulse to devote the rest of his life to tartan research, but some undoubtedly will wish to know more about it and it is for them that this appendix is included. Unhappily there is mighty little else to help them.

The pattern of a tartan is called a **sett** and is given in the form of a **thread count** which sets out the stripes in order and gives the number of threads in each. There are various ways of giving the thread count, but I am here using, as is expedient, the layout which The Scottish Tartans Society employs in its Tartan Register.

Three cases have to be catered for: the ordinary reversing type of pattern, the non-reversing type, and the hybrid form of a reversing pattern with an alternating colour in the overcheck.

The colours are denoted by letters. In general, the initial letter of the colour's name is used:

B for blue	C for crimson	G for green	O for Orange
P for purple	W for white	Y for yellow	

Sometimes adherence to this rule would lead to confusion or clumsiness, in which case other code letters are substituted:

A (azure) for light blue	K for black	
N (neutral) for grey	R for scarlet	T (tan) for brown

A prefix can be used to indicate light or dark shades of colours:

L for light   D for dark

Some colours occur so rarely that it would not be worth having special symbols for them; they are generally named in full on their first appearance in a count and some unambiguous abbreviation is adopted thereafter: lavender can become 'Lav', for example, maroon 'Mar', and so on.

It may be noted that in no case are the colours intended to match any given standard. The use of these code-letters is entirely diagrammatic. Colour in tartan is wholly a matter of art. There are no such things as standard tartan colours.

In a thread count the actual number of threads is quoted rather than a measurement given (but the latter was the method used by James Logan, as described on page 74).

For a reversing pattern, the count is given for the half sett, from pivot to pivot. The *whole* width of the pivot stripes is given. If the end stripes in a thread count are underlined, this indicates that it is a reversing pattern. **Black Watch**, illustrated in Plate 17, facing page 89, is a reversing pattern, and this is the thread count for the half sett:

Black Watch

B	K	B	K	B	K	G	K	G	K	B	K	B
<u>24</u>	4	4	4	4	20	24	6	24	20	22	4	<u>4</u>

Since the full widths of the end stripes are given, we have a blue panel of twenty-four threads at the first pivot, with four lines of four threads all around it, and at the second pivot we have a pair of black lines, each of four threads, with four threads of blue between them.

For a non-reversing pattern, such as **Buchanan** which is illustrated in Plate 3, facing page 56, the count for the whole sett has to be given. In the Buchanan thread count which follows, the three dots at each end show that the sett continues end to end, Y 12 being followed by K 2:

Buchanan

...K	Y	K	B	K	G	B	G	K	B	K	R	W	R	K	B	K	Y...
2	12	2	8	2	12	8	12	2	8	2	16	2	16	2	8	2	12

The design for the **Farquharson** tartan shown in the *Vestiarium Scoticum* is the same as Black Watch, except that the black overcheck on green becomes alternately red and yellow. In the following thread count, the symbol / is used to indicate that the colours alternate:

Farquharson

B	K	B	K	B	K	G	R/Y	G	K	B	K	B
<u>24</u>	4	4	4	4	20	24	6	24	20	22	4	<u>4</u>

So much for knowing what a thread count is about. Now we have to consider taking a count from a specimen.

In the twill weave that is used for tartan, each weft thread passes over two and under two of the warp, so that the weft thread at the edge of a stripe taken in isolation, shows as a series of dashes, each of which covers two threads in the warp, while the spaces between the dashes cover another two. Therefore each combination of dash and space is four threads, and counting along the junction of two contrasting colours is made easy by simply taking four times the number of the 'dash-space' combinations and adding two if there is a dash or space left over. Ten dash-space combinations thus gives us a total of forty threads; dash-space dash-space dash-space dash-space dash-space dash-space dash-space dash, gives us thirty.

With practice, it will be found not at all difficult to take a count of a specimen in a museum showcase, and this method is infinitely easier than counting threads through a magnifying glass. In setting up the loom, the warp is fixed, but the number of weft threads may be varied to square up the pattern, so a count should always be taken in the warp —it is not always possible to distinguish warp from weft, unfortunately, but as a guide, there are often fine spaces between groups of warp threads (occurring where they pass through the reed of the loom) which can be seen if the cloth is held up to the light.

The thread count is the means of *recording* the pattern; the medium for *comparison* of patterns is the **colour strip**. This is no more than the pattern stick interpretation later readers imagined into the remarks Martin made about tartan patterns (page 69) but is executed in poster colour on paper instead of in coloured threads wrapped around a stick. The sections of colour are set out in accordance with the proportions of the thread count. Coloured in, they amount to a short section of the warp as it would appear on the loom; there being no weft, there is no mixture of colours and no confusion in the pattern to blur comparisons.

A subsidiary advantage is that a tartan collection can be kept without the bother of collecting and preserving large numbers of small pieces of cloth.

In making comparisons, we are somewhat hindered by there being as yet no published system for the universal classification of tartans by pattern, but this is on the way to being remedied. Meanwhile, the very act of making and handling thread counts and colour strips will be found to sharpen the eyes and the wits and will lead to many interesting discoveries without too much trouble.

Using colour strips, a large tartan collection can be built up and kept in very little space; the complete Tartan Register of the Scottish Tartans Society, called Sindex for short, occupies two drawers of an 8 x 5 filing cabinet, and the index to that, two drawers of a 6 x 4.

Sindex depends upon a colour-coding system devised by its inventor, Donald Stewart, whose *Setts of the Scottish Tartans* started tartan research in its modern form on its way. It is based on record cards. Each tartan has a card upon which all relevant information is recorded, with a colour strip along the top edge. The colour strip is arranged to cover rather more than one whole repeat of the pattern, and the ends—that is, the pivots in the case of reversing patterns and the start and finish of the non-reversers—are marked. The Sindex code, called the Slog, basically consists of two three-letter groups, representing the first three colours inwards from the pivots of a reversing sett, or a single three-letter group representing the first three colours of a non-reverser; in the former case, whichever group starts earlier in the alphabet goes first and in the latter the group starts with the colour that comes first alpha-betically speaking, and the colours follow on in the alphabetical direction.

The three-letter groups are subject to modification in several ways. If a tartan has less than six stripes, for instance, it is clearly not necessary to have a six-letter slog: a five-stripe tartan has a three-letter group followed by a two-letter group; a four-stripe tartan has a three-letter group followed by a single letter; a three-stripe tartan has a two-letter group followed by a single letter; and a two-stripe tartan has a single letter followed by another single letter.

If a strict application of the rules would result in two reversing-pattern tartans having the same slog, there are three possible solutions to the problem. First, we can go on coding the colours to give us a second group consisting of four or more letters—as many as we need to indicate a difference between the two tartans. If we run out of stripes before we reach a point of difference, we can add a suffix number in brackets after the slog. The third solution is applied when slogging such tartans as the great group of Black Watch derivatives. A repeat of the Black Watch thread count may help to make this clearer:

Black Watch

B	K	B	K	B	K	G	K	G	K	B	K	B
24	4	4	4	4	20	24	6	24	20	22	4	4

This slogs as:

BKB : BKB

The Gordon tartan has a yellow line on the green in place of the Black Watch black so that its thread count is as follows:

Gordon

B	K	B	K	B	K	G	Y	G	K	B	K	B
24	4	4	4	4	20	24	6	24	20	22	4	4

and it slogs as:

BKB : BKB: Y

The *Vestiarium Scoticum* Gordon tartan, which has three yellow lines on the green, slogs as:

BKB : BKB: 3Y

With non-reversing tartans, a similar procedure is applied, the slog being extended as far as is needed to obviate confusion. The Buchanan thread count, as we have seen, is as follows:

Buchanan

...K	Y	K	B	K	G	B	G	K	B	K	R	W	R	K	B	K	Y...
2	12	2	8	2	12	8	12	2	8	2	16	2	16	2	8	2	12

B—blue—is the first colour, alphabetically speaking; G for green precedes K for black, again alphabetically speaking; so this slogs as:

BGKB

As it happens, Buchanan is the only tartan with this slog on the register; if another were to turn up, Buchanan might become BGKBKR (*not*, note, BGKBKY).

Sindex itself requires an index which is in two parts; one lists names and tells what the slogs are, and the other gives the same information in reverse.

Apart from its use as a record-keeping system, Sindex is valuable when tartans have to be identified. It is easy to 'slog' a tartan and it can then be identified, or noted as a previously unknown sett, in a matter of moments.

In the past, slapdash methods have resulted in the recording, and even the making, of many spurious tartans or erratic versions of real ones. The mystique attached to tartan, and the reverence with which it is treated, mean that once an error is made it is almost impossible to put right. The nearest we are likely to come to that is to avoid making any more mistakes ourselves, and even this is a great deal more difficult than one might think. The golden rule is to check, double check, and check again; then, if possible, get a second opinion.

A BOOK LIST

Adam, Frank, *The Clans, Septs and Regiments of the Scottish Highlands*, revised by Sir Thomas Innes of Learney, W. & A. K. Johnston & G. W. Bacon Ltd., Edinburgh and London

Bain, Robert, *The Clans and Tartans of Scotland*, Collins (William) Sons & Co. Ltd., London and Glasgow

Chapman, R. W. (Ed.), *Johnson's Journey to the Western Islands of Scotland* and *Boswell's Journal of a Tour to the Hebrides with Samuel Johnson LL.D.* (combined volume), Oxford University Press, London

Cherry, Eve, *Teach Yourself Handweaving*, The English Universities Press Ltd., London

Dunbar, J. Telfer, *History of Highland Dress*, Oliver & Boyd Ltd., Edinburgh

Grant, I. F., *Highland Folkways*, Routledge & Kegan Paul Ltd., London

Mackenzie, Osgood, *A Hundred Years in the Highlands*

McClintock, H. F., *Old Irish and Highland Dress*, Dundalgan Press, Dundalk

Moncreiffe, Sir Iain, of that Ilk, *The Highland Clans*, Barrie and Rockliff

Scarlett, James, *Tartans of Scotland*, Lutterworth Press, Guildford and London

Scarlett, James, and McBride, Angus, *The Tartan-Spotter's Guide*, Shepheard-Walwyn (Publishers) Ltd., London

Stewart, Donald C., *The Setts of the Scottish Tartans*, Oliver & Boyd Ltd., Edinburgh; reissued, Shepheard-Walwyn (Publishers) Ltd., London

Stewart, Donald C., and Thompson, J. Charles, *Scotland's Forged Tartans*, Paul Harris Publishing, Edinburgh

Thurstan, V., *The Use of Vegetable Dyes*, Dryad Press, Leicester

Wallace, John, *Scottish Swords and Dirks*, Arms and Armour Press, London

The Scottish Tartans Society, The Museum of Scottish Tartans, Comrie, Perthshire, and *An Comunn Gaidhealach*, Abertarff House, Inverness, have published various pamphlets and reprints of magazine articles of general interest to the student of the Highland way of life.

HELP FOR THE INTERESTED

Neither my Book List nor my remarks on places to visit (overleaf) can give much help to the would-be weaver of tartans, for neither takes much account of this specialized branch of the weaver's art; the only way is to acquire the basic knowledge as best one can, and then build upon it from experience, and the best I can do is to offer some information which may be of use.

The book *Teach Yourself Handweaving*, details of which are given on page 117, contains complete instructions for making a small table loom. Drawings showing how to make more ambitious machines are obtainable from The Council for Small Industries in Rural Places, at 35 Camp Road, London S.W.19. The drawings are referenced as follows: P. 22, Swedish-type Loom; P. 24, English Hand Loom; P. 27, Table Loom. Although the making of a loom need not be very difficult, it should equally not be tackled by the totally unskilled.

New looms can be purchased from Harris Looms, North Grove Road, Hawkhurst, Kent. Second-hand looms are very frequently advertised in The Weavers' Journal, published quarterly by the Association of the Guilds of Weavers, Spinners & Dyers, c/o Federation of British Craft Societies, 80a Southampton Row, London WC1B 5BA.

T. M. Hunter Ltd., of Brora in Sutherland, supply tweed yarns in a good range of colours and in 9- and 11- and 16-cut gauges. J. Hyslop Bathgate & Co., of Victoria Works, Galashiels, Selkirkshire, supply a wide range of yarns, including worsted and lambswool.

PLACES TO VISIT

Apart from the City museums, most of which can furnish some matter of interest within our orbit, Scotland can boast many smaller museums that are worth much more than a quick look round.

The West Highland Museum at Fort William and the Inverness Museum are particularly strong on tartans and Jacobite relics; the Clan Macpherson Museum at Newtonmore, and the Clan *Donnachaidh* Museum at Bruar deal adequately with the relics of their own clans.

Highland life of yesteryear can be seen at *Am Fasgadh* in Kingussie, The Angus Folk Museum in Glamis, and Auchindrain close by Loch Fyne, between Inveraray and Furnace. Blair Castle has plenty to show on the same lines, and Jacobite relics and tartan fragments too.

The Museum of Scottish Tartans is at Davidson House, Comrie, Perthshire, and many items relevant to the interests of its parent Society are on display.

For those especially interested in tartans, a visit to the Weaver's Cottage at Kilbarchan is well worth while. Owned by The National Trust for Scotland, the cottage is fully equipped with eighteenth-century weaving apparatus and shows well how the job used to be done.

A map which may prove helpful appears on the facing page.

INDEX

By D. Dainty, M.A.

Note: *Fig.* = Figure; *pl. btw.* = plate between pages x and y; *pl. f.* = plate facing page x